The Hor  's
Guide to

Cedric Meadowcroft

Fourmat Publishing

ISBN 1 85190 023 3
First published June 1987

The Homeowner's Guide to the Law
by Cedric Meadowcroft, Solicitor

Cartoons by Clive Meadowcroft

Fourmat Publishing
27 & 28 St Albans Place   Islington Green   London N1 ONX

Typeset by Pentacor Limited
Printed in England

Foreword

People sometimes ask why lawyers use so much language which is not understood by the public, particularly in legal documents. The answer is that the first priority for anyone preparing a legal document is to avoid ambiguity as far as possible. Regrettably everyday English abounds with ambiguities and double meanings, so lawyers fall back on those words and phrases whose meanings have been clearly expressed by judges in innumerable cases, which, they hope, will avoid any doubt as to what exactly the parties to the document intended to do. Unfortunately the result is that the parties themselves often have to ask a lawyer not only to explain the law on a particular point, but also to interpret the document for them, if problems arise.

In my thirty years as a solicitor I have been asked many times to explain to a client some legal problem relating to his house or other property, "in everyday language and leaving out the legal jargon". This book is an attempt to do just that. It is not a legal textbook, and indeed I have deliberately avoided referring to cases decided by the courts, and Acts of Parliament, in all but a few places. It is, of course, inevitable that a book about the law will contain some special phrases and words which have particular significance in the law. Wherever I have used such words or phrases, which I think might be unfamiliar to the general public, I have briefly explained their meaning in terms which I hope most people will be able to understand. I have also added a glossary of legal terms which might be of assistance to the reader.

Although this book is about houses, or flats, and their owners, it is in no way a "D.I.Y" conveyancer's handbook. It is concerned instead with the everyday problems which the homeowner might encounter and which affect his or her use and occupation of the house. But to people who wish to buy a house or flat, particularly if they should be thinking of doing it themselves, some understanding of the principles of property ownership in England and Wales is a must. I sincerely hope that they, and all other homeowners, will find this book not only helpful and informative, but also interesting.

Homeowners are, of course, both men and women, and it may well be that the majority of houses in this country are now owned jointly by husbands and wives. In writing this book I have generally referred to "the homeowner" as "he", because to have said "he, she, or they" every time would have driven both me, and the reader, slightly mad. Therefore please remember that, as lawyers often say in lengthy documents, "the male includes the female and the singular includes the plural". I still prefer my old French teacher's more elegant version of this: "the masculine embraces the feminine".

Finally I would urge anyone who encounters real difficulties with regard to his home, or anything else, where legal proceedings may become necessary, to seek competent professional advice. Always remember the old adage, "the man who is his own lawyer has a fool for a client".

Cedric Meadowcroft
April 1987

Contents

Chapter 1   **Whose house?**
1 Ownership – an introduction   1
2 Legal ownership and trusts   3
3 Joint owners   6
4 Secret trusts   7
5 Life tenants   7
6 Husband and wife   9
7 Court orders affecting ownership and rights
of occupation   11
8 Transfer of ownership on death   11
9 Acquiring rights of ownership by long occupation   12

Chapter 2   **Leaseholds, ground rents and chief rents**   **14**
1 Freeholds and leaseholds   14
2 Assignment and underlease   16
3 Ground rent   17
4 Chief rents or rentcharges   18
5 Enforcing payment of a ground rent or chief rent   19
6 Sub-rents and apportioned rents   20
7 Extinguishing a chief rent   22
8 The leaseholder's right to purchase his freehold   23

Chapter 3   **Covenants**   **26**
1 What is a covenant?   26
2 Covenants in leases   27
3 Freeholds – Restrictive covenants and positive
covenants   28
4 Who can enforce a covenant?   31
5 Removing covenants from land   32

Chapter 4   **Boundaries**   **34**
             1 The position of a boundary   34
             2 Who owns a boundary fence or wall?   35
             3 Repairing and rebuilding boundary walls and fences   37
             4 Restrictions on erecting walls and fences   38
             5 Boundary disputes   40

Chapter 5   **Rights of way and other rights**   **42**
             1 Rights attached to property   42
             2 Private rights of way   43
             3 Joint rights of way and the responsibility for repairs   44
             4 Rights of light   45
             5 Drainage and the flow of water   46
             6 Rights of support   47
             7 The creation of easements   48
             8 Acquiring rights by long use   49
             9 Infringement of rights – loss of right   50

Chapter 6   **Problems with neighbours**   **52**
             1 Living in harmony   52
             2 Noise, smells, smoke, and fumes   53
             3 Trees   55
             4 Children, visitors and workmen   58
             5 Dogs, cats and other animals   59

Chapter 7   **The flat dweller**   **60**
             1 Community living   60
             2 Common parts and services   61
             3 Freehold flats or leasehold flats?   62
             4 The management of leasehold flats   64

Chapter 8   **Extensions, alterations, improvements and other
             development**   **68**
             1 Planning consent and Building Regulation approval   68
             2 Building works which require planning permission   70
             3 Change of use   72
             4 Building byelaw regulations and the London Building
               Acts   73
             5 Restrictions in the deeds   75
             6 Planning applications by other people   77

	7 Listed buildings and ancient monuments	78
	8 Home improvement grants	80
Chapter 9	**Compulsory purchase and other powers of public bodies**	**83**
	1 Compulsory purchase in general	83
	2 Compulsory purchase procedures	85
	3 Compensation	86
	4 Planning blight	89
	5 Highways and their adoption	89
	6 Smoke control and other restrictions	91
Chapter 10	**Mortgages, rates and other outgoings**	**93**
	1 The nature of a mortgage	93
	2 Tax relief on mortgage interest	95
	3 Powers of a mortgagee	98
	4 General rates and water rates	99
	5 Electricity, gas, and telephones	102
	6 Insurance	102
Chapter 11	**Lettings and lodgers**	**105**
	1 Letting a house	105
	2 Letting one's own house	106
	3 The holiday home	107
	4 The retirement home	109
	5 Letting part of the house	110
	6 Lodgers	111
Chapter 12	**Trespassers, visitors and others**	**113**
	1 Trespass	113
	2 Trespassers before the Courts	114
	3 Self help	116
	4 Burglars	118
	5 Persons lawfully on the land	118
	6 Safety of premises and injury to people who enter them	121
	7 Damage to neighbouring property or passers-by	123
Chapter 13	**A business in the home**	**126**
	1 Working at home	126
	2 Planning restrictions	126

3 Restrictions in the deeds   128
4 Other problems affecting particular businesses   132
5 Outgoings and taxation   133

Chapter 14   **Taxation and the home**   **134**
1 Taxation of the homeowner   134
2 Capital Gains Tax – private residence exemption   135
3 Selling part of the garden   138
4 Husband and wife   140
5 Trustees, beneficiaries, and dependants   141
6 The owner who is not in residence   141
7 The second home   142

Glossary   145

Index   148

Whose house?

1. Ownership – an introduction

In Britain we take pride in the fact that so many homes are "owner occupied". The growth of the building societies movement, unique to Britain, has contributed to our having the largest proportion of owner occupied homes in Europe. But what exactly is meant by "owner"? In any given case real ownership of a house may not be obvious to an outsider because property ownership is something which the owners and their family often keep strictly to themselves. Indeed the owners may not be entirely clear about it themselves, and when questioned about the ownership of their house may give answers like "we are buying it from the building society", or "we own the house but not the ground".

The real ownership of the house is a question of great importance to the vast majority of homeowners for whom the house is not just their single most valuable asset, but is the one possession which is worth more than all their other assets together. Who then truly does own the house, and is that the same as owning the land? Is the owner always the "legal owner"? Are the true owners the couple who live in the house and pay their instalments to the building society, or the building society which provided the money to buy the house? Does the man who collects the ground rent really own the ground?

There are those who would have us believe that English property law is really a very simple matter and that the lawyers make far too much of it. There are even those who believe that English land law is a boring subject. In fact it is a complex system developed over the last thousand years and can be quite a fascinating study. For any one to make sense of the present laws some understanding of the history of land law in England is necessary.

In the Middle Ages land was the only source of great wealth and the major asset of people at all levels of society. The King would reward his loyal dukes and earls by giving them whole counties. They in turn granted large tracts of land to their barons and knights, while the squire, who held the local village as tenant of the knight, controlled the yeomen who were the tenant farmers and cultivated the fields. At the bottom of the feudal ladder came the serfs who were allowed to occupy and cultivate their own small plots in return for working in the fields of their overlords.

In those days land was not the source of wealth simply because it produced income, but rather because it represented power. From the warrior earl in his armour to the yeoman with his longbow who came in from his fields when danger threatened, all the principal tenants were soldiers who could be summoned by the King whenever he needed an army. The word "tenant" in its origin did not mean someone who pays rent for the house he occupies, but a man who "held" his land from his feudal lord in return for military service, and all land owners were tenants ultimately of the King. This accounts for the use of the word "tenant" in ways which at times can be baffling.

The world of course has changed enormously since the Middle Ages and the law has had to change with it. The changes arose at first from attempts to escape from the toils of the feudal system and led to the development of a complex system of minor interests in land and of trusts. From time to time the laws relating to land ownership and trusts have been simplified and codified by various Acts of Parliament but in more recent years a new complication has been introduced, largely as a result of the changed role of women in our society.

All the principal tenants were soldiers who could be summoned by the King whenever he needed an army.

There are now new rights of ownership and occupation which can override the old rules of ownership.

To return to the question of who owns the house and the land, we can say that the true owners are not necessarily the "legal" owners. The person who buys a house with the aid of a mortgage from a building society is nevertheless the owner; while the building society simply has a right to be repaid the loan plus interest. The owner of a leasehold house usually owns the land it is built upon even though he pays ground rent, but his ownership is limited to a fixed number of years. Except in the case of flats or apartments, which are a fairly new concept in English law, the owner of the land owns the ground beneath it, the buildings erected on it, and everything above it. For this reason lawyers when they refer to "land" often mean the house or other buildings on the land. Freehold land is properly called "real property" or as the Americans call it "real estate", but "property" is perhaps the word most commonly used, by lawyers and non-lawyers alike, to indicate land and buildings of all kinds.

2. Legal ownership and trusts

To the man in the street the term "legal owner" usually implies the person who is the true owner, and the one entitled to occupy and possess the property. In the application of the law this is often far from the case. The reason for this seeming absurdity is the development of the trust.

To the tenant who held his land by "knight service tenure", as it was called, the feudal system held some definite disadvantages. Apart from the fact that he could be summoned to drop whatever he was doing, don his armour, or grab his longbow, and hurry out to fight when he really did not feel up to it, there were other things he did not like about the system. There were a number of benefits to the feudal landlord which virtually amounted to a tax on death. On the tenant's death the landlord was entitled to take his best beast. If he left a small son as his heir, then the landlord took over the running of the estate and was allowed to keep all the profits from it until the heir came of age. If the tenant left no son but instead left an unmarried daughter, so much the better for the landlord; he not only ran the estate and took the profits, but also arranged the marriage of the daughter to whoever he wished, and this could often help him to further his political ambitions.

As always when people are subjected to unpopular taxes, they begin to look for ways of avoiding them. The most successful way they discovered was to find two or three friends they could trust and transfer the property to them. They had an agreement then with these friends, whom they called "trustees", that they would hold the property in name only and that the real owner would remain the tenant himself. After the death of the tenant the trustees would keep the property until the son came of age, or the daughter got married, then the property would be transferred back to them. The feudal landlord lost his opportunity to claim his rights because the trustees were then the legal owners. The trust had an added advantage in that the tenant could direct who would have the property when he died, and the trustees would transfer it to them. To many landowners this was a much better arrangement than always allowing the law to take its course. Under the Common Law all the land of a person who had died passed directly to his eldest son, which might be the last thing he would want to happen.

As time went by the schemes became more and more ambitious and the trusts more complicated. From time to time the King and Parliament passed laws intended to abolish trusts or at least limit their effect, but the trust has remained with us and is now an important part of the English land law. Where a trust exists the real owners are the people for whose benefit the trust exists, who can live in the property, or who receive the income from an investment property. Although the trustees are the legal owners they may be simply nominees for the real owners. However, there are many cases where the trustees are also the beneficial owners and hold the property in trust for themselves.

The true owners of the property are called the "beneficial owners" or "the beneficiaries" or "the equitable owners". They are the people who found the money to buy the property even if they borrowed it on a mortgage, or who were given the property by a Will or simply as a gift. The trust may exist because the beneficial owner is a child, in which case the trustees must make all the decisions about the property until he comes of age. However, in most cases the trust exists because there is no single owner of the property but instead two or more people each owning only part of the property. The beneficial owner may be a "life tenant" who owns the property during his lifetime but who cannot give it away by his Will because on his death it passes to someone else named in the trust. At the other extreme the trustees may hold the property on trust for a thousand people who are members of a club or society and who jointly own their club building or sports ground. In each particular case the powers of trustees to make important decisions and the extent to which the trustees' actions may be controlled by the beneficiaries depend upon the wording of the trust document.

How then does one know who is the legal owner? He is the person to whom the property was conveyed by a deed. In lawyers' language the "title" to the property is "vested" in him. The legal ownership can be discovered by an examination of the title deeds.

What then is a deed? Once more we must go back to the Middle Ages in order to understand the difference between a deed and other types of documents. In ancient times very few people could read, write, or even sign their names. Literacy was confined mainly to priests, monks and scriveners (professional writers who would write or read a letter or document on payment of a fee). In those days, when a man putting his signature on a document could not write his name but only make his mark by writing X upon the parchment, nobody would be prepared to accept that he had properly signed it when it had important legal consequences and especially when land was being transferred. Another way of showing that it really was Sir John Smith or Squire Williamson who had signed the document was necessary. Therefore each man of substance would have a seal or a signet ring bearing his own personal device which he would impress upon wax dropped onto the document. To make doubly sure, a witness, usually a man of letters, would sign the document to confirm that he had seen the seal impressed upon it. The distinction therefore developed between important documents which were sealed and those less important which were just signed. The small red paper seals attached to modern deeds may only be symbolic but they provide a convenient way of distinguishing between an important document which will transfer the legal ownership of land and a less important one such as an agreement to transfer the land at a future date.

In more recent times the system of registration of title has been adopted in this country. A government body, Her Majesty's Land Registry, was set up with the object of preparing detailed plans on which the ownership of each plot of land in England and Wales should eventually be shown. There are now District Land Registries in each part of the country at which are kept the plans and registers of owners within that area. There are still a great many people whose ownership of particular plots is not shown on the registers, but little by little new districts are made areas of compulsory registration of title and the plans then begin to be filled with numbered plots, which may be of widely differing sizes, the ownership of which at any particular time is shown in the registers.

After a district has been declared to be an area of compulsory registration, the person buying a house or other property within the district must register his title. The title deeds are sent to the District Land Registry who must be satisfied that the ownership is properly proved. The name of the legal owner is then entered in the register against the number of the plot marked on the master plans. In addition there is a list prepared of leases, covenants, rights of way, mortgages or other matters relevant to the particular plot. But only the legal ownership is shown and no details of any trust appear on the register. On changes of the legal ownership details have to be sent to the Land Registry and the transfer documents, mortgages or other deeds must still be sealed as well as signed to make the dealing effective. The registers are then amended to show the names of the new owners. The privacy of the registered owners is respected, and no-one can inspect the register, or obtain information from it, without the written consent of the registered owners or their solicitors.

3. Joint owners

Joint ownership of houses has been increasing steadily for many years. It is probable that, at the present time, there are more houses owned in the joint names of a husband and wife than those owned by a sole owner. Of course joint owners are not necessarily husband and wife, and as mentioned before all the members of a club may be joint owners of its property.

The first and most important thing about joint ownership is that it always creates a trust. Even when a deed transfers a property to two or more people without mentioning a trust they automatically become trustees. In the vast majority of cases the trustees are also the beneficial owners as in the case of a husband and wife buying in joint names. However the trustees may hold the property on behalf of other people, and this is not necessarily apparent from the deeds. Where the title is registered in the Land Registry only the legal owners, in this case the trustees, will be shown on the register. Even with unregistered land the deeds may not show who are the beneficial owners and this information can be contained in a separate document.

The second important aspect of beneficial joint ownership within the trust is that it may be one or other of two different kinds. True joint owners each own the whole property and when one dies the other automatically owns it all. If they were also the trustees then the trust comes to an end and we are left with one sole owner. The other form of shared ownership is that each owner has a separate share. The shares may be equal or unequal as where one owner provided 75% of the purchase money and the other 25%. In that case if one dies his share does *not* go automatically to the other but instead passes under his Will. The trust therefore does not come to an end on the death of one of the beneficial owners, and if it is one of the trustees who has died a new trustee must be appointed in his place before the property can be sold. If a beneficial joint owner wishes to change things so that on his or her death the whole property will not pass automatically to the other, then he or she may give written notice to the other joint tenant that in future they are each to own separate shares which will pass under their Wills.

Where the deed of purchase states that the purchasers are "joint beneficial owners" or that they hold the property "in equal shares" then on the face of it they are entitled to equal shares in the money when the property is sold. This is so even when one of them has provided more of the purchase money than the other. There is an assumption that there is a gift from one to the other to make their shares balance. This can be particularly important when the purchasers are not husband and wife and may for example cause disagreement in the case of an engaged couple buying a house jointly between them if they should later break off the engagement.

4. Secret trusts

A genuine secret trust occurs when the real purchaser does not want anyone to
know that it is he who is buying. A nominee will buy the property in his own
name with no indication in the deeds that there is any kind of trust. Later of
course the real owner can call upon the nominee to transfer the property to him.
There are however other occasions when a trust of some kind exists without any
formal declaration in the deeds. Usually this occurs within a family and often
without any of them realising that a trust has been created.

It is not uncommon to find that elderly parents pool their resources with one
of their adult children and buy a house between them, but the house is bought
in the name of, say, the son alone. In that case if it is intended that all of them
shall own a share in the house then the son will hold the property in trust for
himself and his parents who provided the money. When the property is
eventually sold the money received by the son as trustee must be divided among
all the beneficial owners in the proportions in which they own it. If the property
is sold at a higher price then the increase is divided between them in the same
proportions. However, in circumstances like this it could possibly be intended
that the son owns the whole house and parents' money has been simply loaned
to him. If that was the intention then all the profit on the sale will belong to the
son.

The entries in the Land Register will show only that the son is the legal owner
even though the father and mother may have a right to receive their shares in the
proceeds of sale. A separate document should be prepared showing the shares in
which they bought the property, but regrettably there are times when there is
nothing in writing to prove it. In that case it may be necessary for the true
position to be proved by other evidence if problems arise.

Decisions in the courts in recent years have established that where, in a case
like this, someone has a share in a property and therefore a right to occupy it, he
or she may have an interest which overrides the legal ownership. For this reason
a purchaser from the legal owner, or a mortgagee wishing to obtain possession
because of non-payment of mortgage instalments, may find that there is
someone in occupation who cannot be forced to leave. The result of this is that
anyone now agreeing to sell a house or raising a mortgage loan will be asked to
obtain the written consent of every adult person living in the house.

5. Life tenants

A person may be given a limited right of ownership which will terminate on his
death or possibly earlier. This is called a life tenancy and the limited owner is
known as "the life tenant" or "the tenant for life". The person who will

eventually receive the property is called "the remainderman" and there may be two or more life tenants who will take the property in turn before the remainderman becomes entitled to it. During his life the life tenant is the true owner, being the person who has the right to live in the house. Life tenancies are most frequently created by the terms of a Will but they may be granted by a deed of settlement.

There are two basic kinds of trust under which a life tenant can hold the property. One is known as a "trust for sale" and this is the same kind of trust as that under which joint tenants own a property. In this trust the legal owners are at least two but not more than four trustees who hold the property in trust for the life tenant who has the right to occupy it. The other kind of trust is known as a "strict settlement" and in this trust the life tenant becomes the legal owner and is the person who has the power to sell or lease the property. In either case if the property should be sold then, unless the money received is used to buy a new house or flat for the life tenant, it must be invested and the life tenant then receives the income from the investment during the rest of his or her life.

The kind of life tenancy which exists under a strict settlement arose from the desire of the landed gentry to keep their stately homes and other lands within the family. The owner of a stately home, wanting his eldest son to succeed him, but being afraid that he may turn out to be a wastrel who will gamble away the family inheritance, gives him only a life interest. The English law used to permit the property to be tied to one family indefinitely by creating an "entail" under which it passed from father to eldest son through each generation, and which was often restricted to male heirs only. Anyone familiar with Jane Austen's *Pride and Prejudice* will remember that the Bennett sisters could not inherit their father's property because it was "entailed" and had to pass to their cousin, the next male heir. This tying up of property for possibly hundreds of years began to have such a stifling effect upon the country that eventually Parliament stepped in and gave the right to anyone in possession under an entailed interest to "bar the entail" which had the effect of making him the sole and absolute owner of the property. This effectively abolished entailed interests so that the landowner wishing to prevent a possible sale, now has to rely on granting a life tenancy which ties up the property for one generation at a time.

Even the grant of a life interest under the modern law leaves a great deal of control in the hands of the life tenant for the time being. The effect of creating a strict settlement is that the legal ownership of the property passes to the life tenant. He can then decide whether to sell it or lease it or mortgage it, and he is the person who signs and seals the deeds. However, the, vital part of the trust is that two or more trustees have to be appointed to look after the money. They cannot prevent the life tenant from dealing with the property as he wishes but the purchaser must pay his money to the trustees and not to the life tenant.

Then if the life tenant buys another house the trustees on his direction pay the money to the vendor. Any money not used to buy a replacement property has to be invested and the life tenant then receives the income.

The more versatile kind of trust is the trust for sale. In this case the trustees are the legal owners and hold the property in accordance with the directions in the Will or deed. The person who creates a trust, called the "settlor", can decide just how much power and control either the trustees or the life tenant shall have. He can direct if he wishes that the trustees will act only upon the directions of the life tenant; or, at the other extreme, he can say that the first priority must be the protection of the property for the remainderman, and give the trustees much more control. Not surprisingly this more flexible type of trust is frequently chosen these days by settlors who wish to grant a simple life tenancy.

One important aspect of the strict settlement to the average homeowner who wishes to grant a life tenancy is that it can be created inadvertently. In particular it tends to arise when people make their own Wills without obtaining legal advice. A Will which states "I give my house to my wife during her lifetime" creates a strict settlement. So do the words "I give my house to my wife for so long as she wants to live there" or "for as long as she occupies it". In these cases a life tenancy is created with the legal ownership passing to the wife until she dies. The intention that the wife should lose her interest in the house if she should wish to move will not take effect.

It is possible to create a trust which will come to the end upon the happening of some particular event but care must be taken in setting up such a trust because the law may override the intention if it should be considered to be against "public policy". A common reason for people granting a life tenancy nowadays is when a second marriage has taken place and the settlor wishes to leave, at his or her death, the house to his or her second wife or husband for life, then on to the children of the first marriage. However it is considered to be against public policy to actively discourage anyone from marrying, so a gift "to my husband for life or until he remarries" will simply give him a life tenancy and the reference to remarriage will be ignored. Even so it is possible by a quaint twist in the law to restrict a life tenancy granted to a wife by stating "I give my house to my wife during her widowhood". In the days before women were considered able to work and support themselves a gift in this form was allowable because it simply made provision for the wife (or it could be a daughter or other female relative) until she married, when the law assumed her husband would provide her with a home.

6. Husband and wife

There was a time when a wife could not own property in her own right. When a woman married she passed the legal ownership of her property to her husband. The very word "husband" originally meant someone who owned and cultivated land.

Once again we go back to the Middle Ages to understand the reasons. When the most important feature of land ownership was that the tenant should be a soldier giving armed support to his feudal lord, a woman was not regarded as a suitable landowner. As mentioned earlier there was a time when, upon the death of a tenant with no son to succeed him, his property would come under the control of the feudal lord who could force the widow or daughter to marry some man of his choosing who immediately became the tenant and legal owner in place of his wife. Surprisingly, although the social circumstances changed hundreds of years ago, the law on land ownership did not change in the same way until just over a hundred years ago when the Married Womens' Property Act allowed a married woman to own land herself.

Whether a house in which the husband and wife live is owned now by the husband, the wife, or jointly between them, they both have a right to occupy it. Most houses bought by married couples in recent years have been bought in the joint names as trustees on trust for themselves as joint beneficial owners. Whoever may have provided the money they each become legally entitled to the whole property, and when it is sold each owns half the purchase money received. If the house has been bought in one name only then it is quite likely that the other can show that he or she made some contribution towards it and therefore has a certain beneficial interest (see "Secret trusts" on page 7).

Even if no contribution can be proved, the husband, or wife, of the legal owner has a right to occupy the house under recent legislation, and that right can be protected by an entry made at the Land Registry if the title to the property is registered, or at the Land Charges Registry if the title is not registered. In the case of a registered title a note is made on the register, just like the entry which gives details of a mortgage, so no-one will buy the house until the entry is removed. An estranged wife (or husband), whose rights of occupation are shown on the register will normally insist upon payment of some of the purchase money to her (or him) before agreeing to the removal of the entry.

For unregistered titles a similar system applies. There is another registry, known as Her Majesty's Land Charges Registry, where entries can be made against the name of any owner of property to protect the wife's or husband's interest, as well as allowing entries to protect mortgages, covenants, etc., as mentioned in later chapters. Such an entry in the register has the effect of preventing the legal owner from selling without the consent of his spouse.

On the breakdown of a marriage the house will be treated as one of the assets of the marriage and, if the husband and wife cannot agree about it, the court will decide for them. At this point beneficial ownership is only one of the factors to be taken into account. After considering all the financial circumstances the court may make an order which will drastically change their rights to the house.

7. Court orders affecting ownership and rights of occupation

The courts, naturally, have the power to make orders affecting the ownership of land. Wherever there is disagreement on the question of ownership, position of boundaries, rights and obligations of trustees or beneficiaries or many other matters, the courts may be called upon to adjudicate and will make decisions which settle the arguments. The courts can also make orders which actually change the ownership of land or the rights of individuals to occupy property, where previously no doubt existed.

In matrimonial proceedings the rights of the husband, the wife or other people may be dramatically changed. Where people are divorced a change in the ownership of the matrimonial home is frequently sought. The courts take into account all the relevent factors including the age of the parties, their income and earning capacity, what other assets they own, the length of the marriage, what each has put into the marriage, not only in monetary terms but also in service to the family, and above all what would be best for the sake of the children. Then a decision is made which can include an order relating to the property. It may be transferred into joint names, or from one of them to the other, or one may be given the exclusive right to occupy it for life, or one may be ordered to sell his or her share to the other at a price which may possibly be much greater or much less than its true value.

In addition to making orders on the ownership of the matrimonial home, the courts may make orders temporarily affecting rights to occupy a house. A husband who has assaulted his wife or children may be ordered to move out of the house and, on pain of imprisonment if he disobeys, to stay well away from it. The fact that he is the sole legal and beneficial owner does not prevent the court from making such an order. Nor is it absolutely necessary for the parties to be married and in these days when a man and woman often live together without being married it is not uncommon for a court to order a man out of his own house leaving the woman in possession.

There are, of course, other circumstances in which the courts may transfer ownership of land, such as upon bankruptcy or to settle a debt.

8. Transfer of ownership on death

Under the old laws of England when land had a special significance, because of the duty of the tenant to provide armed service for his lord, it was treated in a different manner from other possessions when the owner died. In those times the eldest son inherited the land although other belongings might pass to the widow or other members of the family. With changing social conditions, firstly, the owner of land was given the right to make a Will which would direct what was to happen to the land when he died, and eventually land became subject to the same rules as all other assets for the purpose of the modern laws of succession. The owner of land may now make a Will which specifically deals with the land or which simply leaves it along with everything else he owns to the beneficiaries named. If he makes no Will then all his assets pass to his next of kin as laid down in the Statutes.

The legal ownership of land is suspended after the death of the owner and it cannot be sold, mortgaged, leased or otherwise dealt with until probate is obtained. An application has to be made to the Probate Court which makes an order vesting the property in the executors who prove the Will or the administrators if no Will was left. The executors can then themselves sell the property or can transfer it to the beneficiary by a deed called an assent. It is advisable for the assent to be completed before the executors wind up the estate, even if the executors are themselves the beneficiaries, or are named as trustees holding the property on trust created by the Will. If no assent is completed there may be problems at a later date if the beneficiaries or trustees should die before the property is sold.

If the owner who died made a specific gift in his Will leaving his house or other property to a named person, then the ownership of that property is transferred to that person immediately on the death. It is still necessary for the Probate Court to grant probate of the Will and for the executors to transfer the legal estate to the beneficiary before he can carry out any legal dealings with the land himself, but nevertheless it is his. Even nowadays there may be an advantage for the person to whom the land is given by the Will. If the value of the assets of the person who died are insufficient to pay off all his debts, and meet in full all the gifts made by his will, then certain rules come into effect about the priority of the gifts. The land in that case has the first priority after the debts have been settled, and is transferred in full before any other gifts in the will take effect.

9. Acquiring rights of ownership by long occupation

One final way in which the ownership of land may transfer from one person to another is by occupation for a period exceeding twelve years. The occupier can then claim to have a "possessory title" to the property. This is sometimes referred to as "squatters rights". The effect of the occupier's "adverse possession", as it is called, is to extinguish the former owner's right and title to the property. But as usual things are never quite as simple as they appear at first.

Although proof of possession for twelve years will normally extinguish the real owner's title there are exceptions. If the person who is the owner is unable at law to enforce his rights of ownership, because, for example, he is under age, then the occupier cannot become the owner simply by twelve years' adverse possession. When he is able to take proceedings, because in our example he has come of age, the true owner then has six years to claim his rights even if the occupier has had possession for more than twelve years already. However once the occupier has been in possession for thirty years the real owner loses his title to the property altogether.

There is a further problem in that the occupier can only take those rights of ownership which belonged to the real owner he has dispossessed. If this owner was a life tenant then the person who displaces him and occupies the property only acquires a right of ownership until the original tenant dies. On the death of the life tenant the remainderman can claim his property and the occupier must get out.

Similarly a person who acquires a possessory title by occupying property which was held under a lease obtains an interest only for the period covered by the lease. At the end of the period of years granted by the lease the freehold owner can reclaim possession, and the occupier must give up the property just as the real leasehold owner would have been obliged to do. Furthermore the occupier must observe all the restrictions contained in the lease and the rights of neighbouring owners, such as rights of light or drainage, will still apply.

To acquire the possessory title the occupier must be properly in possession throughout the period. He must not make any payment to the real owner or any acknowledgment to him that he is the owner. He must prevent the real owner and everyone else from occupying the property, preferably by erecting fences or walls around it to keep them out. In other words he must act throughout the twelve years or longer period as though he really is the true owner of the property. Anything which indicates that he is there on sufferance, or with the implied consent or approval of the true owners who intend to use the property at some future date but have no immediate use for it, will defeat his claim to a possessory title.

Leaseholds, ground rents and chief rents

1. Freeholds and leaseholds

The legal estates or interests discussed so far have mainly been freeholds. Although in ancient times all owners of land were tenants, holding their land from a feudal landlord to whom they owed allegiance, and who had certain rights to take their land away and give it to another, things gradually changed. As mentioned in the last chapter the ownership of land meant power because the feudal lords each had an army of tenants and subtenants who could be called into service at any time. This made the King feel insecure, because his lords might call out their armies against him, and from time to time they did so. The general public felt insecure because at any time the country might fall victim to warring barons. It was time to curb the power of the noblemen.

By a series of Acts of Parliament, or Statutes, during the Middle Ages, many of the rights of the earls, barons, knights, and other feudal landlords were taken away. One of the most important was the right to create new feudal tenancies which had enabled them to grant tracts of their lands to new tenants, thereby increasing their armies and, of course, their power. This right was abolished in the thirteenth century. As the generations passed and intermediate tenants died, more and more tenants became direct tenants of the King. Their tenancy was called a "feu simple", which became "fee simple", the words still used in legal documents today. The more common name for this is a "freehold", and all freeholders now hold their land direct from the Crown. Being a right to hold the land forever, a freehold interest is, in effect, complete ownership.

Having lost their right to grant new feudal tenancies, the noblemen had to find other ways to make use of their lands. They already had part of their lands tilled by their serfs and villeins, which provided ample food for their households, but what about the rest of their estates? They could sell pieces of land, but what was the use of that? Capital in those days had no real value except for the purchase of other land. They could employ more serfs to till all their fields, but who wanted the trouble of managing vast estates and collecting the

Who wanted the trouble of managing vast estates and collecting the produce for sale?

produce for sale? If they did that they would be no better than the tradesmen they all despised. No, it was better by far to have tenants who had all the trouble and responsibility, and who regularly paid their rent, or risked having their tenancies taken away. The lords could no longer grant feudal tenancies but they could grant tenancies for a fixed period, and indeed a few such tenancies of commercial premises already existed in the cities. So there grew up another form of land ownership for limited periods called leasehold.

A leasehold estate or interest in land is a right of ownership for a period of years. For that period of years the leaseholder has a legal interest in the property similar to the legal estate owned by a freeholder, but the freehold, of course, lasts for ever. In practice a long leasehold is not very different from a freehold. The leaseholder may sell the lease, assign part of it, make a gift of it in his Will, grant another lease for a shorter term, create life interests, trusts for sale, and other interests. He has to pay ground rent, which may be a minor irritation, and, because at some future date the lease will come to an end, he will eventually lose his property unless he can purchase the freehold, or obtain a new lease to replace the old one. But while the lease continues perhaps the biggest difference between a leasehold and a freehold is the way in which covenants may be enforced by the landlord (see Chapter 3).

Leases themselves come in a variety of forms, such as a lease of a private house for nine hundred and ninety-nine years at a yearly ground rent of £10, or a lease of a warehouse for three years at a rent of £10,000 each year. We, however, are interested in the homeowner, and nearly all leasehold houses are held on long leases, usually ninety-nine years, or nine hundred and ninety-nine years. These periods are traditional but originated from the fact that stamp duty, the tax paid on new deeds, varied according to the length of the lease. It is still the case that the stamp duty charged on the rent reserved by a lease for more than a hundred years is twice the amount payable if the lease is for less than a hundred years. If the lease is for nine hundred and ninety-nine years then it is virtually as good as a freehold. The leaseholder will have paid a large capital sum to buy the house, probably with little difference in price between what he has paid for his house, and what his next door neighbour has paid for an exactly similar freehold house. But if the lease were originally for only ninety-nine years, and seventy-five years have already passed since it was granted, then the end of the lease is already very much in sight and the need to purchase the freehold has become an urgent one.

A distinction must be drawn here between the weekly or monthly tenant who has a right of occupation on a week to week or month to month basis, and the leaseholder whose tenancy lasts for years. The weekly or monthly tenant has rights of occupation which are highly protected these days, but he cannot transfer his interest, give it by Will, create a life tenancy or mortgage the land or property as a leaseholder can.

2. Assignment and underlease

Once a lease has been granted the leaseholder has a legal estate which can be passed on. He may sell his whole interest in the property by assigning his lease. Alternatively he may grant an underlease or sub-lease for a shorter term, retaining part of the original term of years so that when the underlease ends the property reverts to him for a time, often just three days at the end of the lease but it may just as easily be nine hundred years. It is in fact most unusual for a single private house sold on a lease to be underleased, but it is commonplace for underleases to be granted of several separate houses when the headlease is a lease of a large piece of land on which all houses have been built.

An assignment is usually a simple sale of the leasehold property, but an assignment of *part* of the property may be made. On completing his purchase of the whole leasehold property the new owner undertakes to pay the ground rent and to perform all the obligations imposed by the lease so that the original owner is then freed from these responsibilities. The landlord must then seek payment of the ground rent from the new owner. However the situation becomes a little more complicated when the leaseholder assigns just part of his lease.

On assigning part of the leasehold land the leaseholder has to decide what to do about the ground rent. He can divide it equally between the part sold and the part retained by him, or make one part pay a smaller or larger share than the other, or even make one part of the land pay the whole rent and leave the other part entirely free. Whatever he does about it the whole of the property remains leasehold under the terms of the lease and is subject to the payment of the ground rent. Unless a legal apportionment is made, as mentioned later, the landlord can call upon the owner of any part of the property leased to pay the whole ground rent due and if payment is not made can send bailiffs in.

When an underlease is granted the tenant of that part of the land, the underlessee, becomes the legal owner of this property for the period of his underlease. The powers granted to him are just the same as those of the head lessor, or intermediate landlord. So he in turn can assign his property, or part of it, or grant yet another underlease for an even shorter term. The underlessee has to pay the ground rent on his own particular property to his own landlord. In addition to paying rent he probably has other obligations imposed by his lease, such as covenants, rights of way and other rights mentioned in his underlease. Again he is subject to further covenants and obligations in the headlease which affect all the land in that original lease. Worst of all if he wishes to buy the freehold of his property he must buy not only the freehold of his part of the land in the headlease but also his own underlease from his immediate landlord; and it may not stop at two. There is no reason why there should not be two, three or more sub-leases.

3. Ground rent

Ground rent probably became so called because with the expansion of urban areas land owners began to lease pieces of land to builders often requiring no lump sum payment, but simply reserving a rent. This way the builder obtained this land at, effectively, no cost to him. He built houses on it which he then sold, and he passed on the responsibility for the rent to the new houseowners. They would have underleases with rents payable to the builders, and, when all the houses had been built and sold, the builder would collect enough ground rent from his tenants to pay the head ground rent, and often to leave him with a handsome surplus. The rent therefore was originally charged for a piece of ground, but as lawyers consider the land to include the buildings on it the term does not denote a rent on the ground as distinct from the house. It is in fact a useful term to distinguish this kind of small rent under a long lease from the full value rent paid on a commercial lease which is called a "rack rent".

The amount of ground rent payable under a lease in usually a fixed sum each year throughout the whole of the term of the lease; but not necessarily so. Because of the high rate of inflation in recent years there are some modern leases, particularly of flats, which provide for the rent to increase every few years. Generally the increase in such leases are of fixed amounts, for example a lease for ninety-nine years may state "during the first thirty three-years the yearly rent shall be £25. During the next thirty-three years the rent shall be £50 and during the final thirty-three years the rent shall be £75". At least in such a case the new tenant can see just what he will have to pay in future, but some leases provide for the rent adjustment to be based upon the future retail price index or some equally unpredictable factor. However the type of rent adjustment clause of which a prospective tenant should be most wary is a clause which relates the future rent to the "market rental value" of the property. Very occasionally one comes across a lease which makes a provision such as "for the first twenty-five years the yearly rent shall be £25, for the next twenty-five years it shall be the market rental value of the property . . . ". The effect of such a clause may well be to convert a ground rent of £25 at the end of twenty-five years into a rack rent of £4,000 a year for the next period. Instead of buying an asset which will increase in value the tenant of such a property would find the value falling rapidly as the time for the rent adjustment approaches.

The payment of ground rent, as well as providing an income for the landlord, also keeps the landlord and the tenant in touch with each other throughout the lease. The tenant will always know who the landlord is, or at least who are the agents acting for the landlord, so there can be no doubt about who will be entitled to the property when the lease expires. If the tenant wants to buy the freehold he will have no difficulty in finding the freehold owner, and there can be no doubt about who can force the tenant to perform his covenants.

4. Chief rents or rentcharges

There is another way of producing income from land although for some reason it never became popular in England except in one or two relatively small areas. The rentcharge as it is correctly called, or the chief rent as it is commonly known, is a rent which is payable out of freehold land. In certain areas of the country, and in particular in and around Manchester, the chief rent has in the past been widely used. The majority of houses in Greater Manchester are freehold but subject to the payment of a chief rent. However it is a dying form of interest in land.

The creation of chief rents was the solution devised by some enterprising landowners to the problem of obtaining a rent when the prospective purchasers did not want to take a lease. The landowner therefore sold the land, but on condition that there should be a rent payable by the owners of the land forever. To both the owner of the land and the owner of the chief rent the effect is similar to a ground rent on leasehold land but of course, the ownership of the land does not revert to the original owner.

A chief rent owner is treated as though he were a landowner. The chief rent can be sold, mortgaged, made subject to a trust or settlement or otherwise dealt with like a house or other land. As with a ground rent a chief rent may be divided between parts of the land, and this frequently happened when a builder bought a large piece of land subject to a chief rent then, having built several houses on it, he sold each separately. Again the builder could create a new rentcharge on each house as he sold it so that he collected the various rents and remained responsible for paying the head rent. Once more as in the case of leaseholds the owner of the house may find that there is a sort of pyramid of chief rents with his house at the bottom and three or four tiers above all charged in part upon his land.

The importance of chief rents is rapidly decreasing because they are being phased out. Since 1977 it has not been possible for anyone to create a new one and in 2037 they will simply disappear overnight when all rentcharges are to be abolished.

5. Enforcing payment of a ground rent or a chief rent

In the case of both a ground rent and a chief rent the rent is payable whether the rent owner demands payment or not. In practice the rent owner, or estate agents acting on his behalf, usually send out demand notes each half year requesting payment of the half year's instalment, but if no demand is received the owner of the property should make the payment anyway. Most ground rents or chief rents are paid "in arrear", which means that each payment is for the period ending on the date when payment is due, but occasionally the rents are stated by the deeds to be payable in advance, in which case the payment is for the period following the payment date. It is the usual practice in England and Wales for the payments to be made each half year and for this to be paid on two of the usual quarter days, 25th March, 24th June, 29th September and 25th December. There is of course no magic in these dates and the deed creating the rent may just as easily say that the payments will be once a year on the first of May.

If the payments of ground rent or chief rent are not made on the due dates then the rent owners can enforce payment in a number of ways. For both ground rents and chief rents the powers given to the rent owners are much the same.

The usual method employed is called "distraint", which means sending in the bailiffs. The rent owner does not need to make an application to the court but simply completes a form instructing the bailiffs to collect the rent, and they then call at the house to demand payment of the rent due, plus their fees for collecting it. If the homeowner is unable to pay them fully in cash, then the bailiffs will sieze whatever goods, furnishings, or other moveables they find at the house which can be sold to raise the money needed to pay off the rent and costs. When things have reached this stage it is no use offering the bailiffs a cheque because a cheque could bounce. However they will usually wait at the house while the money is obtained from a bank if this can be arranged.

The second method of enforcing the ground rent or chief rent is to collect the rent from anyone who is obliged to pay rent to the person owing the ground rent or chief rent. For example A sells a house to B on a lease subject to a ground rent of £10 a year (or sells the freehold subject to a chief rent of £10 per year). B lets the house to C, a weekly tenant, for £5 per week. If B does not pay the ground rent (or chief rent) to A, then A can call upon C to pay the weekly rent direct to him until the ground rent has been fully paid. If C is not a weekly tenant but has a sub-lease from B, then A can ask C to pay his ground rent direct to A.

If the property is not sub-leased or let then A may himself let it to a tenant and charge him rent until the ground rent due to A is paid in full. In practice this way of collecting an unpaid ground rent is very rarely used and really it is only a possibility if the property is completely unoccupied.

On the grant of a lease a right is automatically given to the landlord to re-enter the property and terminate the lease if the ground rent is not paid. Although there is no such right automatically granted to a chief rent owner, the deed creating the chief rent often gives him a similar right to sieze the property back if the rent is not paid and if the bailiffs cannot find enough goods on the property which can be taken to cover the debt. Again in practice there is rarely any attempt to forfeit a property in this way, and the owner can always save the loss of his property by paying the rent which is due and the rent owner's costs in full.

Finally the rent owner may make an ordinary claim in the courts for the unpaid ground rent or chief rent. Usually, however, he finds it easier and quicker to obtain payment by one of the other methods and particularly by sending in the bailiffs.

6. Sub-rents and apportioned rents

As previously mentioned the first ground rent or chief rent on a property has often been created when a large piece of land was sold to a builder. After building several houses on it the builder has sold the houses one by one, and the responsibility for the ground rent or chief rent has been passed on to the house purchasers. This result may have been achieved in one of several ways.

Imagine a situation where a builder purchased a piece of land as a site for ten houses. The original landowner granted a lease to him subject to a yearly ground rent of £200. Having built the ten houses, the builder may have sold each one subject to the payment of a yearly rent of £20 as part of the original ground rent;

so when all ten have been sold the whole rent is paid by the new owners, and the builder no longer has any interest in it. On the sale of the last house the last part of the headlease was assigned to the purchaser of that house, who then became responsible for collecting the part rents from the other nine houseowners, and for the payment of the whole of the rent of £200 to the landlord.

Alternatively the builder might have decided to remain responsible for the payment of the rent of £200, but to collect a new rent from each of the new houseowners, leaving himself a margin of profit. In that case he could have granted underleases to each purchaser, creating new ground rents of £30 on each house. The builder then collects £300 a year from the houseowners, and pays £200 to the head lessor, keeping the difference for himself.

If the builder bought freehold land, subject to a chief rent, then the situation is not very different. Again he may have sold each house subject to part of the original rent, or may have created new chief rents on each sale, leaving himself a margin of profit. However no new chief rents can now be created, as all chief rents are being phased out. The builder, or other landowner, owning property subject to a chief rent, and now wishing to sell off a part subject to a new rent, must grant a lease on which a ground rent can be created.

The effect of dividing the rent is that, in our example, the builder must collect the part rent from each new house and he continues to pay the whole rent. When the last house is sold the last part of the rent becomes payable by the last purchaser but he must also take the responsibility for collecting all the other parts and paying the whole amount to the rent owner. This can be a terrible burden to an ordinary houseowner, who probably does not like even to ask his neighbours for their share of the rent, let alone threaten to send in the bailiffs if they will not pay him.

Fortunately there is a way out for the unlucky owner who bought the last house. He can make an application to the Department of the Environment for a legal apportionment of the rent. This applies whether the rent is a ground rent or a chief rent. The person applying must complete a form giving full details of the rent payable and how it has been divided between the various houses. The Secretary of State for the Environment will then sign an order dividing the rent into a number of separate rents. The rent owner in future must collect each part separately and can no longer demand the whole rent from any single owner.

Unfortunately this power given to the Secretary of State, to divide a ground rent or chief rent into separate rents, will not apply if sub-rents have been created instead of the original rent being shared out. Usually, in the case of sub-rents being created, the total of those rents is greater than the head rent so that the person who collects them makes a profit. The person who has to pay the head rent probably does not live in any of the houses, but simply has an interest in the property either as a head leasehold tenant who has granted shorter sub-leases, or as the person who owns the sub-chief rents. In either case the owner of the head rent, if he cannot collect it from the person responsible for payment, may still call upon the houseowners to pay him direct until he has received payment in full. If the person who has to pay the head rent does not wish to collect the other rents himself, then the fact that he has a profit margin on the rents usually allows him to employ an estate agent to collect the rents for him.

7. Extinguishing a chief rent

A chief rent may be brought to an end in several ways, the first of which is by the homeowner buying it from the rent owner at a price they agree. If this rent is just part of a chief rent paid on several houses then the homeowner buys a release from his part of the rent. When the rent owner and the homeowner have agreed upon the price, the rent owner must prove his title to the rent by producing his deeds. The deeds are examined and a purchase deed then prepared, signed, sealed and completed just as though a piece of land were being sold.

It is advisable for the homeowner to instruct a solicitor to deal with the purchase of the rent, and as the agreement usually includes paying the costs of the rent owner's solicitor as well, the total costs are often considerably more than the price being paid for the rent. This is not because the solicitors are rogues, but because the price to be paid is usually very small, while the solicitors must charge for the time they spend investigating the title and preparing and completing the deed.

In most cases where the chief rent is to be bought by agreement the original suggestion has come from the rent owner who wants to rid himself of this troublesome asset and invest his money in something better. The homeowner being asked if he would like to buy his rent often thinks the idea is a good one, but he should beware of paying too high a price. The value of a chief rent as an investment is well below the figure which homeowners are sometimes asked to pay, and in these days of high interest rates no-one should consider paying more than seven or eight times the amount of the rent. In addition, the homeowner may not at that stage realise that he will also be expected to pay the legal costs which will often be more than double the cost of buying the rent.

What then should the homeowner, who would also like to be rid of this vexatious, if not generally very expensive, liability for rent do about it? Once more we return to our old friend the Secretary of State for the Environment. The homeowner can complete a form applying for the rent to be extinguished; the Secretary of State sends a notice to the rent owner, asking him to prove his ownership, then makes an order extinguishing the rent on the payment of the price which he fixes. The price is decided according to a formula based on the value of certain government stocks at the time, and usually works out at about seven times the rent.

In the event of a chief rent being unpaid for more than twelve years it can become extinguished. The chief rent owner who fails to enforce payment of the rent will lose his right to it, just as the owner of land may lose his title to the property if he allows someone else to occupy it for twelve years. However the chief rent will not be extinguished if the rent owner is collecting the rent from someone else, even though the owner of the land has paid nothing during the last twelve years. Also the period of non-payment may be longer than twelve years, without the rent being lost, if special circumstances apply as in the case of squatters' rights (see page 12).

If no steps are taken to extinguish a chief rent, then in August 2037 it will cease to exist. The Rentcharges Act 1977 states that all rentcharges (i.e. chief rents) will then be abolished and will simply cease to be payable.

8. The leaseholder's right to purchase his freehold

Until 1967 the owner of a house on a long leasehold, subject to a ground rent, had an interest which lasted only to the end of his lease. When the lease expired he had to move out and hand the house back to the freeholder. Once into the last fifty years of the lease the property became difficult to sell, building societies were reluctant to grant mortgages, and the value steadily fell. But in 1967 the Leasehold Reform Act was passed by Parliament and everything changed.

A leaseholder who has owned his house for five years, and lived in it throughout that period, usually has a right to buy the freehold; but as always there are exceptions. Only a house which fits the following conditions will qualify:-

(a) It may be detached, semi-detached, terraced or a back to back house, but, for the purpose of this particular Act, a flat is not a house, nor is a residence which has a material part projecting over or under another person's building. A garden, garage and other outbuildings are included with the house.

(b) The lease must be a long lease at a low rent. A long lease is one for more than twenty-one years. There is a formula for calculating what is a low ground rent but for most houses it will be less than £100 a year.

(c) The lease must be within certain value limits, again calculated on a formula related to old rateable values, but the effect is that generally only very large and expensive houses will *not* qualify.

(d) The leaseholder must be the owner occupier at the date when he makes the claim; it must be his only residence or his main residence; he must have lived in it as his only or main residence for at least five years out of the last ten years. However, if the leasehold owner dies and a member of his family who lives with him then becomes the owner, the period of ownership and occupation of the person who died can be added to that of the new owner to arrive at the total of five years.

Assuming that a leasehold owner qualifies under the rules he can then force the freeholder, and any intermediate leasehold owner, to sell their interests to him so that he becomes the freeholder himself. The steps he must take are as follows:-

(1) He gives written notice to his landlord by completing a form and sending it to the landlord, and also a copy to the head landlord, if there is one.

(2) The landlord can then demand that he pays a deposit (not more than £25), and also that he proves his ownership of the leasehold interest and the period during which he has lived there.

(3) When satisfied on this the landlord must confirm that he will transfer the freehold to the tenant, and he then says what price he wants. If they cannot agree about the price after some negotiation, they can ask a body called the Land Tribunal to fix a price which will then be binding on both of them.

(4) Once the price has been fixed the landlord (and also any head landlord with whom a price will also have been agreed or fixed by the Land Tribunal) must transfer the freehold to the leaseholder. The leaseholder must pay the price which has been fixed, whether he likes it or not, or withdraw completely if the price is more than he can afford.

The disadvantage of this procedure is that a leaseholder who begins by serving a notice on his landlord will be committed to paying all the costs and expenses of the landlord as well as himself from that moment. It may be weeks or months later before he knows just how much the freehold is going to cost him. If he does then wish to back out because it is more than he expected he must still pay everyone's costs which could prove very expensive. So what should he do first?

The first step which a wise leaseholder will take is to contact his ground landlord, or the landlord's agents, saying that he is thinking about the possibility of buying the freehold. He should ask whether the landlord would be prepared to sell, and what price he would want. Most landlords arrange for their ground rents to be collected by an estate agent who has some expertise in these matters, so the leaseholder is likely to be given a good indication of the sort of price he will have to pay. The landlord's agent will know that the tenant can force the sale anyway, but, in putting a price upon the freehold, will probably ask a little more than he expects to get. The leaseholder can then decide whether he wants to press on with his proposal to buy the freehold.

There is no easy way for the person who is not an expert to say, in general terms, what a reasonable price might be for a freehold reversion. Except in the case of a very long lease, with hundreds of years to run, it is likely that the leaseholder will be asked to pay a much higher price to rid himself of a ground rent than he would to buy up a chief rent. However the price for the freehold, even when there are only a few years left to run, will be very much less than the price he would have to pay to buy the same house, freehold, with vacant possession. Of course the price goes up as the lease nears its end, and anyone owning a leasehold house with less than fifty years to run should seriously consider buying the freehold as soon as he can afford it. When the lease is into the last twenty years the situation is becoming extremely urgent. It is also a factor that when into its last fifty years a leasehold house becomes very difficult to sell, unless the freehold can be bought in, and a leasehold owner who wants to sell his house will probably be forced to buy the freehold in a hurry and, quite possibly, at a higher price than he would otherwise have to pay.

Having enquired about the price and still wishing to buy the freehold, whether he thinks the price asked is reasonable or not, the leaseholder should next obtain professional advice before he commits himself further. He should ask a solicitor to advise him about the proposal generally, and find out what the legal costs are likely to be. If he, or the solicitor, believes that the price the landlord has asked for the freehold is too high, but he is still anxious to buy it anyway, then he should consult a surveyor or estate agent and ask for his advice on the price. The surveyor will, if so instructed, negotiate with the landlord's agents to see if a price can be agreed between them and, if necessary, give evidence on his behalf to the Land Tribunal when the question of the price is referred to them.

The Leasehold Reform Act gives the leaseholder another option. He can, if he wishes, apply for an extension of his lease rather than purchase the freehold. The lease will then run for a further fifty years, although the ground rent will be adjusted to take present day values into account. The lease cannot be extended in this way more than once, but leaseholders who have extended their leases in this way can later enforce the sale of the freehold.

3

Covenants

1. What is a covenant?

Most homeowners will have come across the word "covenant" but may not understand its exact significance. When buying their house they are likely to have heard from their solicitor that the property is subject to certain covenants affecting its use. If they have a mortgage then they will have noticed that in the mortgage deed they have covenanted to pay the mortgage payments. What then is a covenant and how does it differ from a condition, an agreement, a restriction etc?

A covenant is a solemn and binding undertaking. The ancient Israelites made covenants with the Lord, solemn promises which under no circumstances would their consciences allow them to break. This idea of a special binding undertaking, along with the word "covenant", was adopted by the laws of England, and a special set of rules gradually developed making covenants quite different from mere promises, which are not by themselves legally enforceable. The idea of a covenant binding upon the conscience of the man who made it, called "the covenantor", was eventually extended so that in certain circumstances it could become binding on the conscience of others who knew about it and accepted it, although they had never actually given the covenant themselves. To be fully effective a covenant must be under seal, i.e. contained in a deed (see page 4 for the meaning of a "deed").

In general under the English law an agreement, or contract, will only be binding upon the two people who make it if each gives something to the other. For example there is a binding agreement if A promises to sell his car to B, and in exchange B promises to pay A £500. If A promises to give B his old car when he gets his new one next week, but B does not give or promise anything to A in return, then, although A may consider this promise binding on his own conscience, it cannot be enforced at law. However if A signs and seals a deed of covenant promising to give the car to B, then the law will force him to do so. Similarly if A makes a covenant in a deed that he will not erect any building in his back garden, then B can prevent him doing so by asking the courts to make an order to stop him. Given the right circumstances B can also prevent C, who later buys A's property, from building on the back garden.

2. Covenants in leases

Tenant's covenants and landlord's covenants have been an important aspect of leasehold ownership ever since leases first began to be granted. In the early Middle Ages leases were always for what is now regarded as a short term, and it was considered to be impossible for a lease to exceed forty years. In those days the leases were much more like modern business leases at a rack rent, and the tenancy existed only between the landlord and the tenant personally. Covenants by the tenant were included in leases, not only to cover the payment of rent, but also to ensure that the property was kept in repair and good order for the landlord when he took it back at the end of the tenancy. In return the landlord would covenant that, provided the tenant paid his rent, he would be allowed to occupy the land without disturbance, and that the landlord would protect him from any outsider claiming that he had an interest in the property. In addition each of them might include several other covenants about erecting and repairing fences, allowing access to the land and so on.

In time landowners began to grant longer leases because they felt that the tenant would have more incentive to plan for the future, and invest time and money in long term improvement projects, if he knew that the land would still belong to him and his family when the benefit of the improvements could be enjoyed. With the lengthening of tenancies the transfer of ownership of both the leasehold interest and the freehold interest became of increasing importance. Not only was there an increase in the number of cases where either the original tenant or the original landlord died during the term of the lease, but also it became more common for one or the other to wish to sell his interest in the property, conveying the freehold, or assigning the leasehold, to someone entirely outside the original agreement.

The judges of the day, applying common sense to the situation, developed new rules of law to allow efficient management of land. Althought the original covenants by both the landlord and the tenant had been personal undertakings, the courts decided that a new tenant taking over the existing lease, or a new landlord acquiring the freehold, would inevitably know what covenants were in the lease because they would each receive the copy of the deed of lease from the original tenant or the original landlord. Each of the new owners must therefore accept both the burden and the benefits of the covenants in the lease. A tenant who had purchased the lease could force the landlord to perform or observe his covenants, but in return he could be forced by the landlord, whether he were the original landlord or someone who had purchased the freehold, to pay the rent and perform the other tenant's covenants. These rules are now incorporated in the modern statute law regulating the rights of landlords and tenants, so both positive and restrictive covenants remain enforceable, when either the leasehold or the freehold changes hands.

3. Freeholds – restrictive covenants and positive covenants

The position with regard to covenants on freehold property is very different. Covenants on freeholds fall into two basic categories, positive covenants, and negative or restrictive covenants. Positive covenants are undertakings to do particular things, for example, covenants to build walls, to construct roads, or to keep buildings in repair. Negative covenants, or as they are usually called, restrictive covenants, are imposed to prevent certain actions, for example, not to erect buildings on a piece of land, not to carry on a business, or not to keep pigeons on the property. The positive covenants have to be "performed", and usually cost money, the restrictive covenants must be "observed", and require no action by the covenantor.

Usually covenants affecting freeholds are made when a property is sold. In most cases it is the purchaser who enters into covenants, which again are personal undertakings, to do, or to refrain from doing, something upon the property he has bought; but sometimes it is the vendor who gives covenants affecting the land which he has retained. The "covenantor" (i.e. the person who has given the undertaking) must do as he has promised, and can be forced to perform his covenant by an action in the courts if necessary. As covenants are binding on the person who has made them, he remains responsible even after he has sold the property to which they relate. Although he may then be unable to carry out the covenants himself, no longer owning the land, he can be made to pay compensation if the covenants are broken. For this reason it is customary for a person selling land which is already subject to covenants, to ask the purchaser to enter into a new covenant with him to perform those earlier covenants. This enables the original covenantor to make the person who bought the land from him perform the covenants, or pay the damages which a court might award, if the person entitled to the benefit of the covenants later sues him for breach of covenant.

For hundreds of years this was the legal situation with regard to all covenants on freehold property. But it was unsatisfactory for the "covenantee" (i.e. the person who has the benefit of the covenants), because he might well have to be satisfied with a payment of money by way of damages, rather than being able to force the present owner of the land to perform or observe the covenants as had originally been promised. If a man owning a handsome country house sold off

It was no compensation to receive money as damages when a future owner of the land built a glue factory on it.

some land close to his house subject to a covenant that nothing would be built upon it except a private dwelling-house, then it was no real compensation to him to receive money as damages when a future owner of the land built a glue factory on it. In those days, before there were any town and country planning controls, such covenants could be very important indeed for the well-being of the whole neighbourhood. And this was not the worst of it, because even a claim for damages could only be made for so long as the original covenantor was alive. As soon as anyone in the chain had died, the personal covenants could no longer be enforced, and there was no way that anyone could bring pressure to bear upon the new owner of the land.

The breakthrough came in 1848. Some forty years earlier a Mr Tulk, the owner of valuable properties fronting Leicester Square in London, had sold the land in the middle of the square, and the purchaser had covenanted to keep it as an open garden and not to erect any buildings upon it. Years later the property was sold and eventually a Mr Moxhay who then owned the square, began to build upon it. Mr Tulk was furious and applied to the Chancery Court for an injunction to prohibit Mr Moxhay from building on the square. Mr Moxhay openly admitted that he knew about the covenants made by his predecessors, but said they did not affect him, and he could not see how anyone could prevent him building on his own land. He was wrong though. The court decided that as Mr Moxhay knew that any building on the square had been prohibited by the covenant given to Mr Tulk, then it would be against his conscience to build upon it. He was made to retain the square as a garden.

Once this decision had been made other cases rapidly followed and a new set of rules was developed for freehold covenants. The courts were not prepared to enforce positive covenants against a new owner, forcing him to do something positive which he had not himself promised to do in the first place, but they would stop him from doing something which had been prohibited by the earlier covenants. However, the restrictive covenants would not be enforced against someone who later bought the land and who genuinely did not know that such restrictions had ever been placed upon it. In practice such ignorance was very rare indeed, because the deeds still regularly contained covenants by the new purchaser for the protection of the man selling and to relieve him of liability once he had parted with the land. Even if the latest deeds did not contain such covenants for indemnity, the courts decided that a purchaser should be assumed to have knowledge of the covenants if by making the proper and reasonable enquiries he would have learned about them.

The situation with regard to covenants on freeholds remains basically little changed. Positive covenants will still not be enforceable against a new owner of the property, except by an action against the original covenantor who in turn can force the man who bought from him, provided he also entered a covenant to perform those earlier covenants. Provided that each purchaser in turn gave a covenant to his vendor, and all are still alive then the present owner may still have to perform the covenants.

A restrictive covenant may also be enforced by proceeding against the original covenantor in the same way, but alternatively may be enforced by an action against the present owner of the land. For a restrictive covenant to be enforceable against the present owner of the land, who was not the original covenantor, the following conditions must apply:-

(a) The covenant must be a negative one. The important thing here is the basic nature of the covenant, not the form of wording used in the deed. For example a covenant which states "the purchaser will not allow the buildings to fall into disrepair or the garden to become overgrown", is a positive covenant even though set in a negative form. The purchaser has to perform this covenant by repairing the house and working in the garden. On the other hand a covenant "that the purchaser will use the land as an ornamental garden only", is a negative covenant meaning that he will not build a house upon it or use it for a car breaker's yard.

(b) The purchaser must have notice of the covenant. If the purchaser knew or should have known about the existence of the covenant then he is bound by it. Since 1925 it has been necessary for *new* covenants to be registered in the Land Registry or the Land Charges Registry if they are to be effective against future owners. Once the covenant has been registered all future owners are regarded as knowing about it.

(c) The person seeking to enforce the covenant must be the owner of other land which will benefit from the covenant.

(d) The covenant must be specifically related to the land in question, and this is a necessary ingredient of covenants in leases also where they are to affect a future owner. For example, a lessee of a public house, who entered into a covenant that he would not open another public house within half a mile, was making a personal covenant only which did not directly affect the public house itself. When he assigned his lease the new owner was not bound by the covenant.

4. Who can enforce a covenant?

The landlord who grants a lease retains an interest in the land itself (i.e. the freehold reversion which will bring the land back to him when the lease ends). The covenants by the tenant are clearly for his benefit and will pass to whoever becomes the owner of the freehold in future. Therefore it is the present owner of the freehold who will be able to enforce the covenants. Similarly the owner for the time being of a chief rent (see page 19) will be able to enforce, against the owner of the land, covenants which were attached to and intended to protect the value of the chief rent.

Where a covenant affects freehold property and is not attached to a chief rent, then, if it is to be really effective, and especially if it is to affect future owners, it must exist for the benefit of neighbouring land. The person imposing the covenant is usually selling just a part of his property and the covenant is intended to protect the value of the rest of the land which he is keeping. When he sells that other land, or parts of it, the people who buy it will usually also take the benefit of a restrictive covenant which they can enforce, if necessary, by making an application to the court. The courts will normally uphold the covenant by granting an injunction which will prevent the covenantor, or later owners of his property, from using it in a way which is a breach of the covenant. In the case of a building estate there is quite often a "building scheme" under which all the houses are given the benefit of all the restrictive covenants on every other house, so that each future homeowner on the estate can enforce the covenants against every other homeowner.

If there should be a breach of covenant there are several ways in which the person benefiting from the covenant may seek to enforce it. Firstly he may apply to the court for an injunction to make the covenantor perform or observe his obligations. The court can order that the covenantor must do certain things, or allow the person who has the benefit to enter on the land and perform the covenants himself for which he can claim repayment of the costs incurred. Alternatively the person aggrieved might seek monetary compensation for the breach. In the case of a lease, and in some cases where property is subject to a chief rent, there is another powerful weapon in the armoury of the landlord or chief rent owner. For a serious breach of covenant he can claim forfeiture of the lease or a transfer back to him of the property. Fortunately for the houseowner he can avoid this drastic consequence by asking the court for "relief from forfeiture" but he must then promptly carry out all his obligations under the covenants and pay the landlord for the costs incurred.

5. Removing covenants from land

Covenants attached to leasehold land are usually brought to an end when the leasehold owner buys the freehold of the property; but not necessarily so. If there is a simple purchase of the freehold, whether by private agreement or after an application to the Secretary of State, then the two titles merge into one freehold and the covenants simply disappear. However it is possible for the freeholders to make it a condition of the sale of the freehold that certain restrictive covenants will be kept, and in that case they are stated again in the deed transferring the freehold to the tenant. Even when the sale is a compulsory one, ordered by the Secretary of State under the Leasehold Reform Act, it can be made a condition that the restrictive covenants remain in force if the freeholder still has property nearby, including other properties which have been leased, which benefit from the restrictions.

The leasehold owner need not necessarily buy the freehold just to discharge the covenants. If he wishes to be released from a particular covenant he may ask the landlord to discharge that covenant and if the landlord agrees a deed of release will be signed and sealed. Usually in such circumstances the landlord, if he is agreeable, will require a payment for releasing the covenant.

So far as freehold properties are concerned, the owner of the land subject to the covenant can similarly negotiate with the owner of the land which has the benefit to release the covenants or a particular covenant. Another way in which they may be discharged is by one person becoming the owner of both the properties.

The difficulty for a person wishing to be freed from covenants on his land is to be sure just who is entitled to enforce them against him. When the covenants have been in force for a long time, and many properties are affected by restrictive covenants imposed more than a hundred years ago, then it can be hard to discover who now has the benefit. Very often the land intended to benefit from the covenant has been sold in several plots, all of which may have succeeded to the right to enforce the covenants. However, if the freehold owner whose property is affected by the covenant, begins to use the land in a way which is prohibited by the covenant and no-one claiming to have the right to enforce it seeks to prevent him, then in time the covenant will lapse.

There is an alternative procedure for discharging covenants. If the area in which the property is situated has changed to such a degree that the covenant is no longer reasonable or applicable then the owner of the property may apply to the Lands Tribunal to discharge the covenant. This can happen for example when a house, which is subject to a covenant not to use it for the purpose of any business, is in what was once a high class residential area, but has now become a commercial area with most of the large houses converted into offices. In such a case the Lands Tribunal can release the owner from the covenant but may direct that he should pay compensation to any persons who can show that they will lose by this.

Boundaries

1. The position of a boundary

It is unfortunately a fact that for the majority of private houses in this country the correct position of the boundaries is not clearly defined in the title deeds. Many houses, especially older terraced properties, have no plans with their deeds. For many more, the plans simply show a large piece of land, originally sold to a builder as the site for a large number of houses. Those title deeds to houses which have a plan, showing the position of the land relative to roads and other major features, frequently state that the plan is "for the purpose of identification only", which means that it is only intended to give the approximate position of the plot and may not even be to scale. Even those properties where the deeds contain a plan showing detailed measurements of the length of each boundary, do not always provide the perfect answer because they may not show at all the house which has been built on the land. If they show the house, which is probably the only solid and immoveable object in relation to which the position of boundaries can be calculated, there is often no guarantee that the site of the house itself is drawn to scale or correctly sited on the plan. It is therefore no surprise that boundary disputes can be most troublesome problems for both the owners of the properties concerned and their solicitors.

It is with regard to boundary problems that the rules about possessory titles (see page 13) become of real importance to a very large number of homeowners. For most houses the position of the boundary is usually decided, initially, when the builder marks out the plots by erecting fences, or at the least by knocking posts into the ground at intervals then linking them with a heavy wire stapled to each post. Prospective purchasers looking at the building site can see from the start just where their gardens will be. Walls and fences are built and hedges are planted along the lines indicated by the builder's markers. The boundaries are well established for all to see, and after twelve years the plots within those boundaries have become the true property of the owners by right of possession, despite any inadequacy in the deeds, or indeed even when the boundaries so established do not coincide with what the deeds show. Perhaps surprisingly it is unusual to find disputes or problems with regard to boundary positions in these early stages.

Another stage in the establishment of the true boundary position is reached when the title to the property is registered in H.M. Land Registry (see page 5 as to registration of title). At this time the boundaries are surveyed by the Government surveyors, the exact position of the fences, walls and hedges are plotted on master plans, and the entries in the land registers for each property show the boundaries then existing. The Land Certificate for each plot then shows the plot drawn to scale. However it is still open to any owner to dispute the position of the boundaries shown in the land register if they do not coincide with the deed plans, and provided that it can be shown that the present walls and fences have not been standing there for twelve years. Also there are occasions when the plans in the Land Registry will show a piece of land not included within the boundaries of any of the adjacent properties, if the walls and fences on the ground are clearly not in the position shown in the deed plans. In that case the plan of the house on one side will show the boundary at the position of the actual fence, while the plan for the house next door will show the boundary in the position where it is shown on the deed plans, leaving the doubtful piece in between as no man's land. The person claiming that the missing piece of land really forms part of his property must then prove to the satisfaction of the Land Registry that the plans should be amended and if necessary the wall or fence moved.

Even when the property has been surveyed and included in the Land Registry's plans there can be some difficulty in establishing the exact position of the boundary. Unfortunately the plans prepared by the Land Registry and shown on the Land Certificate are of too small a scale to show the detailed position to anything more accurate than about a foot. Sometimes it becomes necessary to know where the boundary lies to within two or three inches, as in the case of someone erecting a garage at the side of his house where there may be only just sufficient room to fit it in. Such a situation can give rise to a boundary dispute.

2. Who owns a boundary fence or wall?

The deeds to any particular house may well contain detailed directions about who is to erect the walls and fences and afterwards keep them in repair. Sometimes in a building estate the erection of suitable fences or walls is included in the price paid for the houses, and the builders then put them up as the houses are built and sold. Often however, the duty to erect a fence is placed firmly upon the purchaser. Once put up the fence or wall is regarded as being owned by the person who constructed it and future owners of his property. On inspecting title deeds it is commonly found that the person who first bought the land to build a house, or the builder buying a large area of land for an estate, entered into a covenant that he would erect suitable fences around it. Within modern housing estates it is usual for the individual house purchasers to enter covenants to erect and afterwards maintain and repair particular walls and fences around their plots. It is customary for the boundaries which are to be the responsibility of the purchaser to be shown on the plans marked with a 'T' projecting into his property. Usually therefore each owner becomes responsible for building and repairing the walls and fences at one side of his land and possibly at the back.

With older houses a different arrangement generally exists, and particularly with terraced houses. The walls and fences are stated to be "party walls and fences" which means that they are the joint responsibility of the two owners who share them. This is obviously necessary with the separating walls of the houses themselves and in modern town houses or semi-detached houses those walls are made party walls even though the garden fences along the same boundary belong to one owner or the other.

Party walls are said to be jointly owned but, except in Greater London, they are regarded by the law as divided vertically down the middle. Therefore although the brick or stone structure of the wall itself should be repaired at the cost of the two owners jointly, the inner surfaces, the plaster, the wallpaper or paint, remain in the ownership of the separate dwellings. Also for this reason there is no restriction upon the owner of a semi-detached or terraced house attaching shelves, kitchen units, built-in wardrobes or other things to his own side of the joint wall.

Party walls between properties in Greater London are a special case, being controlled under the London Building Acts. These walls are indeed jointly owned by the owners of the properties on both sides. Because of this anyone owning a property in London who wishes to carry out work on the party walls, including such things as underpinning, cutting into, thickening, repairing, building onto, or pulling down and rebuilding, must first give formal notice to his neighbour of his wish to do so. On the credit side for the homeowner in London is the fact that he has a right to do any of those things provided that he follows the correct procedure under the London Building Acts, and pays whatever is the appropriate part of the cost of any such works, including both owners' surveyors' fees and any other incidental expenses. Basically the costs are all payable by an owner who wishes to do work purely for his own benefit, but are to be shared if the work is necessary repair work which will benefit both properties. As there are often elements of both self interest, and necessary repair, in any proposal, the costs and expenses are not necessarily shared equally. Any owner in Greater London wishing to do work affecting a party wall should first consult a competent building surveyor who will guide him through the intracacies of the procedure, and negotiate with the neighbour's surveyor on the question of the costs.

3. Repairing and rebuilding boundary fences or walls

It is easy to say that the owner of a house will be responsible for keeping a particular fence in repair, but much more difficult to make him do so. The building and repairing covenants are, of course, positive covenants, and so are difficult, if not impossible, to enforce against a future freehold owner. Even in the case of a leasehold housing estate, the owner of one house would be unlikely to persuade the landlord that he should take steps to enforce the performance of such covenants against the next door neighbour.

Then there is the question of personal choice about the kind of boundary fences to be constructed. Mr A., who is responsible for building a particular fence, may like an open aspect across the back gardens of the neighbours, and therefore intends to erect a two foot high chain link fence. His next door neighbour, Mr B, likes to protect his privacy and wants Mr A to put up a six foot high close boarded fence. Obviously in this case Mr B cannot force Mr A to build the sort of fence that Mr A would object to, but what happens when the two of them have joint responsibility for a party fence?

As must be apparent, there has to be a great deal of toleration and co-operation between neighbours, if they are to avoid conflict over the question of boundaries. In practice most homeowners will discuss with their neighbours their ideas about repairing or replacing fences before they actually begin to do anything. Very often the two owners will agree upon the type of fence, and will also share the cost, even though the deeds may direct that one of them owns the fence in question and is responsible for the whole expense of maintaining it. If this kind of relationship exists the neighbours are likely to live in peaceful co-existence with each other.

Unfortunately there are times when the two owners not only fail to see eye to eye in the first place, but are not prepared to compromise and try to reach an amicable agreement. If the man responsible for the fence, or for a share in the cost, will not repair or replace it then his neighbour may be forced to do the work himself at his own expense. If the disagreement goes deeper, as in the example of Mr B wanting a six foot high fence which will block the view of Mr A, then Mr A may refuse to allow Mr B to replace the old fence with such a large fence, even if Mr B intends to pay the whole of the cost. In that case if Mr B remains determined to have his high fence he can still put it up but it must be on his own land. There are many examples of this around the country when the true boundary is still defined by an old, perhaps dilapidated, fence or hedge, but one of the neighbouring owners has built a new sturdy fence inside his own land and a foot or so from the original one.

So long as the old fence or hedge remains to mark the boundary line there can be no doubt that the true boundary is still on that line and that the new fence is on the land of, and clearly owned by, Mr B. However the situation is unlikely to stay like that forever. At some time Mr A, or some new owner who has by then bought his house, will become tired of the sight of the old rotting fence posts or the dying pieces of privet hedge. He will pull them out and extend the flower bed up to the new fence. He may also wish to mask the unsightly fence by training climbing plants against it. In the meantime Mr B, secure behind his barricade, is unlikely to notice, or even to care, what is happening on the other side of it, and probably will never think to raise objections. Twelve years later, when both properties may well have passed into new hands, Mr B's splendid fence will become the legal boundary because his neighbour will be able to show that the extra strip of land became part of his garden and has been in the undisputed possession of himself and the former owners of the land for the necessary period.

4. Restrictions on erecting walls and fences

There are certain restrictions on the size or type of walls and fences which may

Mr B, secure behind his barricade, is unlikely to notice or even care what is happening on the other side of it.

be built, and there may be a prohibition upon erecting one at all. The restrictions are basically of three kinds: restrictions in the deeds, restrictions imposed by the Town and Country Planning Acts, and restrictions which the Courts might impose to protect other people's rights of light. Certain restrictions imposed by the Planning Acts are of general application, and can only be amended by obtaining planning consent, while others are imposed as part of the conditions attached to a particular planning consent. In addition there are a few cases in which the liability to fence is imposed by statute and is therefore much more effective than any private fencing covenants.

Private restrictions may be contained in the title deeds to a house. These will of course be restrictive covenants and therefore enforceable against future owners. When found in deeds such restrictions are usually about the type of fence or wall which may be built, and its maximum height. For example a covenant might state that "no fence shall be erected in or around the garden except a chain link fence not exceeding four feet in height". In modern housing estates there are often restrictions about building fences walls or hedges of any kind in between the house and the road. These are generally included in the deeds because the local planning authority have decided that the housing estate should be what is known as an "open plan" estate, and the restrictions in that case are more likely to be enforced by the Council than by neighbouring owners.

Planning restrictions may be included in the general planning consent for the particular property or as a part of the planning law. In addition to placing restrictions on all fence building in an open plan estate, a restriction frequently imposed on corner properties is for the protection of "lines of sight" at road junctions. For the sake of road safety a homeowner may be prevented from building a wall or fence, or even allowing hedges or bushes to grow, within a certain distance of the corner of the road. Such restrictions are likely to be rigidly enforced. There is however a general restriction on building any wall or fence more than two metres high or, if it adjoins a highway, more than one metre high. If the homeowner has some good reason for building a higher wall or fence he can apply for planning permission to put up a wall or fence of the particular height he wants.

The other major restrictions on wall or fence building is to prevent the interference with rights of light to a neighbouring property (see the next chapter as to the grant of such rights). If the owner of a property has a right of light to his windows, then any neighbouring owner may be prevented from building walls or fences or growing hedges or trees which will partly shut out his light and darken his room.

The duty imposed on a landowner by Act of Parliament to put secure fences around his property does not normally affect the homeowner directly, but may permit him to make sure that certain boundaries are kept in repair by someone else. This duty falls principally on the railways, who must fence their tracks to prevent children or animals straying onto them, and upon county highway authorities, who have a similar responsibility for motorways and trunk roads. A homeowner whose garden is bounded by a railway or motorway can insist upon British Rail or the County Highway Authority replacing or repairing their fences whenever necessary.

5. Boundary disputes

Disputes over boundaries are best avoided. They can be long drawn out, very expensive, and, as it is rare for anyone involved to feel wholly satisfied with the final outcome, they usually result in the two owners involved feeling much more bitter towards each other at the end than they did at the beginning. They are the sort of cases about which people say that only the lawyers can win, but even lawyers do not like them. To the lawyer they are troublesome, time consuming, and often leave him with a dissatisfied client, which no lawyer ever wants.

Most boundary disputes arise over one of the problems mentioned earlier; the position of the boundary, the height of the fence, and who must pay to repair or rebuild it. As this chapter has been devoted to the various problems relating to boundaries there is not much to add about disputes except, perhaps the most important of the disputes, those relating to the boundary position. The basic difficulty in dealing with a dispute over the position of the boundary is the generally inadequate definition of the boundary positions in the deeds of a house. When disagreement arises it is frequently many years after the house was originally built and its garden fenced. The fences may have been blown down or rotted away. What hedges or fences remain may equally well be upon the true boundary line or on either side of it, and very often the people who built the fence or grew the hedge have moved away years ago so that no-one living there can now positively say what actually happened. It therefore becomes necessary with the aid of whatever plans may be available, the services of an experienced land surveyor, and a large measure of common sense to try to establish just where the boundary should now be.

In most cases a real dispute is unlikely to arise about any major error in the boundary position, which on investigation must be fairly obvious, except possibly a dispute about whether one owner has established a right by occupation of more than twelve years. The disagreement therefore is often limited to a question of a relatively small difference in the possible boundary position. This has probably become of crucial importance to one owner because he needs the extra space to build a garage between his house and the boundary, or because he has a driveway barely wide enough to take his new car past the house to his garage at the rear. In such cases a successful outcome to a claim may justify the high expense incurred, but to anyone considering entering into expensive litigation with his neighbour because he considers it to be a "matter of principle" the advice must be to forget it. Where the exact position is a matter of real importance it is far better to negotiate a payment to the neighbour for his agreement to the adjustment than to embark upon a course which will lead to litigation.

Rights of way and other rights

1. Rights attached to property

The homeowner will usually benefit from a variety of rights, while his neighbours have the benefit of certain rights affecting his property. There are public rights and private rights; natural rights and rights which have been granted specifically; permanent rights and temporary rights. The differences between these various rights may not always be apparent and calls for some explanation.

To begin with public rights are those which the public at large benefit from and are not particularly attached to the homeowner's property although he will benefit from them. The most significant to the homeowner is the right to use the public highways to get to and from his house (see page 89 as to highways).

Secondly there are certain rights which are referred to as natural rights and which are automatically attached to all properties. Examples of these are natural rights of support which prevent anyone from cutting the ground away from under one's property, and the right not to be disturbed in the peaceful occupation of one's house. The latter right is covered by the law of "nuisance" and is mentioned in Chapter 6.

Then there are temporary or personal rights granted to the present owner by neighbours. These are called "licences" and may be granted by a formal document or by an informal oral arrangement between friends. There are no really technical rules about such licences, each of which depends upon the particular arrangement. An example would be oral permission given to the homeowner by his friend, who lives in the house backing onto his, to cross his friend's garden as a shortcut to the railway station. This right is personal to the homeowner, and can be withdrawn by the friend at any time. It is certainly not intended to pass to anyone who buys the homeowner's house.

Finally there are the private rights which become permanently attached to a property. These are called "easements" and are by far the most important rights so far as the ownership of property is concerned. An easement, once attached to a property, becomes part of that property and passes to all future owners of the property. All easements are rights over neighbouring properties and are normally granted by deed. In the remainder of this chapter the various rights mentioned are easements unless another kind of right is specifically mentioned.

2. Private rights of way

A private right of way is given to the owner of a property to cross the land of another in order to reach his own property. Although the right generally includes the right for other people with his permission to walk or ride to his house it is still his right and only he can object or take action if anyone is prevented from reaching his house. The grant of a right of way is usually contained in the title deeds to a property, but such a right can be acquired by long and undisturbed use or, very occasionally, because it is a "right of necessity". There are some private houses which are reached by a private road which has never been made a public highway and of course rights of way over that road are usually set out in detail in the deeds to a house saying what kind of traffic can use the road, and who is responsible for repairing and draining it. The vast majority of private houses have access to the house or garden direct from a public highway, and for most of these any private rights of way are for secondary access over the passages crossing adjoining properties. The one type of property which usually does rely on private rights of way for all access is the flat, which has rights of way in common with other flats in the block over private roads and footpaths.

Most private rights of way attached to houses are rights to gain access to the rear of the houses over passageways or drives which are often used jointly by several owners. Again the rights to use the secondary access road or passage are usually set out in reasonable detail in the deeds and shown on plans attached to the deeds, but for many older terraced houses there are no adequate plans with the deeds and the rights of way are by implication only. Nearly all terraced houses built in the nineteenth century or early twentieth century were built as investment properties to be let to weekly tenants. Many of them are still let to tenants, but since the end of the First World War large numbers of them have been sold to owner occupiers. The deeds of sale of the individual houses may mention particular rights of way, but often in the past such deeds contained rather general terms referring to the continued enjoyment of "all easements and quasi-easements" relating to the property. Quasi-easements are rights which are like easements and which have been enjoyed between tenants or other occupiers of properties which all have the same owner. If there should be a disagreement about what rights were given to the purchaser of a house by such general words, then it would be necessary to ask the former tenants of the house in question to make statements about what rights had been given to them when they lived there. Information from neighbouring owners about the use of such roads or passages is also extremely important, especially if the former tenants of the house have died.

A right of way of necessity is very rare anyway and hardly ever applies to private houses. It exists where the deed fails to give any rights of way but without some right of way there is no possible access to the property. In that case a right of way over other land of the person who sold the property had to exist to make it reachable, and the law therefore assumes that a right of way was granted by the vendor who simply forgot to mention it in the deed.

3. Joint rights of way and the responsibility for repairs

The majority of rights of way to private houses are joint rights shared between two, or several, houses. The most common form is a right over a road or passage leading to the back of a row of terraced houses and shared by all the owners or occupiers but passing outside the back yards or gardens. The ownership of such a passageway is generally unimportant. As all of them have an equal right to use it, going to and from their homes, they will usually be jointly responsible for keeping it in repair. The deeds will usually say that the owner of each house will contribute a fair proportion of the cost of repairs. If the deeds make no reference to repairing the passageway then the responsibility for repairs is decided by the law which makes the person who benefits from a right of way responsible for keeping it in repair, so we are back to the same situation. It is possible for the deeds to specify that the costs of repair shall fall upon the owner of the land over which the passage runs, or upon some particular user of the rights, but this is most unusual. The question of whether the passages belong to one particular person or are divided between all the owners, who each own the strip adjoining their garden, is therefore generally unimportant; at least it is until Marks and Spencer wish to buy up the whole site and build one of their shops, when the number of square yards owned by each resident becomes a matter of great importance.

The other major kind of rights of way, the mutual rights over a passage between two houses, poses different problems. In this case the rights have usually been granted long after the houses were built, although there are some new houses for which joint drives were provided when they were built. Many houses were built last century or in the early part of this century before the ownership of a motor car became common and the passage down the side of each house was no wider than was necessary to accommodate a wheelbarrow. In recent years with the increase in motor car ownership it has become a regular arrangement for the dividing fence to be pulled up and the two passages converted into one drive which gives access to garages built in the rear gardens of the houses. When a car drives along the drive it is crossing both properties at once. It is normal for a deed to be drawn up granting mutual rights of way over the combined drive but there are still houses which exercise such rights on an informal basis. When deeds are drawn up they may state that the whole of the combined drive is to be repaired at the joint expense of both owners but otherwise each owner probably remains responsible for just his own side of the drive.

Although the general rule about positive covenants is that they cannot be enforced against a later owner (see page 30), the situation with repairing rights of way is somewhat different. The right is usually made conditional on the person using it keeping the road or passage in repair or, where appropriate, paying a proportion of the cost of repairs. In this case if the repairs are not made, or the price is not paid, then the person in default may be prevented from using the road or passage until he has paid up.

4. Rights of light

There is no natural or basic right to light. A right of light only exists where it has been granted to, or acquired by, the owner of a property. If it is a permanent right attached to the property it is an easement. An easement of light, or, as it is

The person in default may be prevented from using the passage until he has paid up.

sometimes called, a right of ancient lights, is a negative easement. It is the right not to have the light shut off from one's windows. As always it is much easier to state what the right is than to say how it is applied, or when there is a breach of the right.

To be able to claim the right at all a person must show that he has a building which has been illuminated by daylight coming through windows or other apertures. Normally the right is granted to the owner of a house who is entitled to have sufficient light coming in through his windows for the comfortable use and enjoyment of the property as a house. The right can be attached to some buildings of other kinds but the right cannot be claimed for all buildings. A garden shed for example, could not be said to have a right of light.

Even when the right is clearly attached to a house, it can be most difficult to decide whether the right has been infringed. There are no fixed rules for deciding how much light ought to come through a particular window. The owner of the house is certainly not entitled to have the full amount of light so that no-one can put up any structure which will block out any part of the light, but the person building on the adjoining plot must make sure that he does not put his building too near the window, or build it so high that he shuts out a substantial part of the light. Each case must be decided entirely on its merits and it can be a very difficult judgement as to whether a new building, or an extension to any existing one, will block out so much light that the neighbouring owner no longer has the comfortable use and enjoyment of part of his house during daylight hours.

5. Drainage and the flow of water

In ancient times the right of a landowner to have water flowing to and from his land was very important. Water might be brought onto his land to water his cattle or irrigate his crops, or drained from his land to prevent it from flooding. In order for the flow of water in or out to be recognised by the law as an easement, or right, which could be enforced against neighbouring owners the water had to flow within defined channels, that is, brooks, streams, ditches or culverts. These rights still exist today, particularly in country areas, but for the average homeowner the importance of these rights is in clean water coming in through the water pipes and foul water going out through the drains and sewers. These days electrical cables, gas pipes, and telephone wires in addition to water pipes, and drains, are all connected to most houses and sometimes cross other people's land to get there. Of these, drainage is the most likely to affect neighbouring properties because of the unique problem it suffers from; that it must run downhill. There is a second problem which has affected the development of modern drainage systems; that the main sewers are of wide gauge and every connection into them is a potential point of weakness. Most main sewers are laid under the roads and are owned and kept in repair by the local authority. To keep down the number of connections into these sewers it has been the common policy throughout the last fifty or sixty years for most housing estates to be constructed with combined drainage schemes. The drains for several houses will be grouped together into a common drain which usually runs through the front gardens, but may be at the rear if the lie of the land makes that necessary, and the common drain has just one connection into the sewer. The owners of the houses are then all jointly responsible for the repair of their combined drains. Upon any fault occurring in any part of that combined drainage system, including the common drain itself and all the drainage pipes leading to it from the individual houses, the owners of all the houses are responsible, usually in equal shares, for the cost of cleaning, repairing, or, if necessary, replacing the drainage system or any part of it.

Although it is the local authority which is in general responsible for the repair and maintenance of the public sewers, the owners of the houses along the road may be responsible for sharing the cost of those repairs also.

6. Rights of support

There are two kinds of rights of support, the natural right of support which all properties have, and easements of support which are granted to or acquired by particular properties. If the man next door digs a pit in his garden close to your boundary, as a result of which your land begins to sink, or tilt, or slide toward the pit, then that is a breach of your natural right of support. If, on the other hand the man next door pulls down his semi-detached house as a result of which your house, deprived of its support, begins to lean, or even collapses, then there is only a breach of a right of support if you can show that you had obtained an easement of support.

When the owner of a building has obtained a right of support for that building then the neighbour who does anything which causes a loss or reduction of that support will be liable to pay compensation for any damage caused. If there is no right of support for the building, the neighbour cannot simply demolish his house without caring whether damage is caused to the other house, but must use reasonable care to make sure that he does no damage. However, if the simple withdrawal of support by the removal of the house by the neighbour allows the remaining house to lean or sag he is not obliged to shore up the walls. But in pulling down his house the neighbour must not do anything to damage the party wall between the two properties which has to be left whole in order to complete the remaining building.

7. The creation of easements

Those rights attached to property known as easements, and which are of particular interest to the homeowner, usually come into existence in one of three ways. The first and most obvious is by deed where the right is set out in detail or referred to in general terms. Even when no rights are specifically mentioned in the deed this right may be implied, which is the second method. Thirdly the right may be acquired by usage over a long period.

Easements granted by deed may be granted to the purchaser of part of the property owned by the vendor. The deed will often set out in detail certain of those rights, such as a right of way over a road or passage, whether it is a footway only, or what vehicles might drive down it. Other rights may be granted by reference to another deed, as when it refers to the arrangements for drains in a separate combined drainage agreement. Yet more rights may be in general terms such as a statement that the vendor grants to the purchaser "the rights in the nature of easements previously enjoyed by the occupier of the property over adjoining or neighbouring land of the vendor", which would, for example, give the purchaser rights of light to existing windows and rights of support from adjoining buildings. Similarly the deed may grant rights to the vendor for his adjoining property over the land which is being sold, and it is most likely that the same deed will both grant rights to the purchaser and retain rights for the vendor.

Then the rights may be granted by one landowner over his land for the benefit of a neighbouring owner. A good example of this is the grant of mutual rights of way over a combined drive between the houses as mentioned earlier. Another example is the grant by one owner to his neighbour of a right to have a telephone wire crossing his land to the nearest telegraph pole. Such deeds will usually set out the rights granted in detail, and limited to very particular rights.

Easements granted by implication only apply when part of the property owned by the vendor is sold. This most commonly happens when the owner of several houses, previously let to tenants, sells one which has become vacant. If no mention is made of any rights then the law assumes that the purchaser takes the benefit of existing passageways previously used by the tenant of the house, light coming in through the windows, and so on. It should be noted however that the vendor does not get any implied rights over the property sold in such a case. Also it is not uncommon to find a deed stating specifically that a particular right is *not* granted to the purchaser, and especially a builder often states that no rights of light are granted or implied which would prevent him building on neighbouring plots.

8. Acquiring rights by long use

Proof of long and unhampered use can establish legal rights over land but based on rather different principles from those creating a right of ownership mentioned in Chapter 1. The principle upon which a person can acquire a right of way, a right of light, or some other easement attached to his land was established many hundreds of years ago. It is based upon the assumption that if someone has behaved as though he truly has a certain right, and has done so for as long as anyone can remember, then the right must have been properly granted to him and his behaviour over such a long period is simply proof of this. It was said in such cases that the right had been exercised "since before the time whereof the memory of man runneth not to the contrary". Evidence would be given by the oldest inhabitants of the village who could say that they had always known that the right was enjoyed.

Now we come to another strange quirk in the English Law. In the year 1275 an Act of Parliament, known to us as the Statute of Westminster, set a date upon the time which was considered to be the limit of legal memory. The date fixed was 1189, the year in which Richard I came to the throne. Afterwards anyone wishing to prove that some right had existed within the memory of man still tried to prove it by evidence given by the oldest inhabitants of the village but if it could be shown that the right could not have existed since 1189 because, for example, the house for which a right of light was claimed had not been built before 1189, then the claim must fail. For some inexplicable reason the limit of legal memory has never been changed and even today it is necessary for someone claiming a right on this ground to show that it could have existed before 1189. There are of course not too many houses standing today which were built eight hundred years ago.

As always when faced with a dilemma like this the judges, exercising their common sense in order to develop the Common Law, devised a new method of proving the existence of an easement. They began to assume that if it could be shown that someone had used a roadway or some other benefit for his property for very many years then there must have been a deed granted which has since been lost. Everyone knew that "the lost modern grant", as it was known, was really fictitious, but it became accepted as a legitimate way for someone to claim a right based on long and undisturbed use. Eventually Parliament had to do something to rationalise the position and laid down new rules for claiming such rights in the Prescription Act 1832. Under this Act anyone who can show that light has been coming through for twenty years has an enforceable right of light, except where such rights are excluded by the deeds or in writing. Similarly rights of way, water, and support can be proved by showing twenty years' use or forty years' use. There are certain defences which can prevent these rights being claimed after twenty years. In particular the fact that the owners of the land over which the right is claimed were under age, or were of unsound mind, or proof that oral consent had been given, may defeat the claim. After forty years these defences will not prevent the right becoming accepted as a full legal and enforceable right. Surprisingly the old methods of claiming rights by long use were not abolished by the Prescription Act which simply added the new basis for a claim. Occasionally, even nowadays, the old methods of establishing that a right exists can still be of some use.

Anyone claiming a legal right over the land of a neighbour based on long use must show that:-

1. The use has been continual, throughout the period of twenty years or forty years as the case may be, and that at no time has the owner of the land prevented him from exercising it for longer than one year.
2. That at no time has he exercised the use by force.
3. That he has not had the landowner's permission, and after forty years simply that he did not have written permission.
4. That in the case of a right of way he has not exercised it secretly.

The essence of any claim to have a legal right which is based on long use is that the use has been enjoyed "as of right". In other words the homeowner claiming that a right exists has to be able to show that he and the previous owners have been using the passageway, or enjoying light through their windows, as though a legal right had already been granted to them. Anything which suggests that they were acting with permission, or in secret, or had allowed the way or the light to be blocked without protest, will defeat the claim.

9. Infringement of rights – loss of right

If the homeowner is prevented from enjoying a right of way or other right attached to land then there are certain things he can do. First he may apply to the Court for an injunction ordering the person to stop whatever is interfering with the right, for example a neighbouring owner may be ordered to stop building, or to pull down a wall which will block the light to a window, or to remove a fence he has erected across a passageway. Secondly the homeowner may himself pull down the fence blocking the passage, or enter on the neighbours' land to pull down the wall blocking his light, but first he must give adequate notice of his intention to do this and he must not cause a breach of the peace. Thirdly, in an emergency he may act without giving notice, as, for example, in the case of a blocked drain causing flooding of the drainage system, or by removing an obstruction from the private road when it is preventing the fire engine getting to his house which is on fire. Fourthly he may claim compensation in money for the loss of the right.

Generally it will be most unwise for the homeowner to take physical action to remove an obstruction or other infringement of his rights. He should give written notice of his intention to do something about it and if the neighbour does not put the matter right then he should consult a solicitor about what action he may take. Whatever he does he must avoid putting himself in the wrong by taking some action which is likely to lead to a breach of the peace, i.e. a fight or other physical confrontation. In any case direct action can only be taken if the right is already a legally established one and not just one claimed because of long use. Unless the right is clearly granted in the deeds to his house, or has already been confirmed by an order of the Court, then any direct physical action by him could be disastrous because he will have used force which may prevent him claiming that the right exists.

Once a legal easement does exist then it may be lost again if the owner abandons it. The fact that he stops making use of it for a time or allows someone to interfere with it without protest will not necessarily cause the right to be lost, and there is no fixed time limit after which such a right will come to an end. However if it appears that the owner has abandoned the right, then the Court may decide that it has ceased to exist. The length of time during which it has not been used may be important, but the intention of the owner is what really matters. An owner who uses a particular room as a darkroom for several years may not have abandoned the right of light to the window, but if he bricks up that window then he will be assumed to have given up the right. A right of way no longer used, because the owner has another exit which he always uses, is not necessarily abandoned, but if he builds a fence across it and cultivates a flower bed in front of the fence then he has shown his intention of giving up the right of way.

6

Problems with neighbours

1. Living in harmony

As with disputes over boundaries, so we can say of disputes with neighbours in general: they should be avoided at all costs. There are few things more ruinous to the happiness of anyone than to live in a state of cold war with the next door neighbour. Living in harmony with the neighbours, like living in harmony within a family, can demand a great deal of give and take, of tolerance and understanding, but making the effort is always worthwhile. Considerations of principle, or loss of face, should not be allowed to get in the way of an attempt at an amicable agreement over any problem with a neighbour. If one person, feeling irritation over some action of his neighbour, once allows himself to retaliate by doing something designed to annoy the neighbour, then the trouble between them can escalate quickly to the point where life for one or both becomes unbearable. When this happens there is seldom any satisfactory outcome until one of them moves house.

Disagreements between neighbours are, of course, unavoidable at times. Often they begin, or are made worse, by the ignorance of one or both of them as to the legal rights and wrongs of the situation. Sometimes one person becomes angry because he feels that something the neighbour has done is a serious infringement of his rights, when in fact no such rights exist. On the other hand one of them may quite innocently do something which he thinks is his right, but which is in fact a serious breach of his neighbour's rights. There is no harm in discussing the problem with the neighbour in a friendly manner, but before any serious confrontation develops a person needs to be very sure of his ground. Above all he should not take any retaliatory action but, if the matter is serious enough, should seek legal advice about what he might do.

Many disagreements with neighbours are over boundaries as mentioned in Chapter 4, but there are some other common causes of dissent. Noise, smells and fumes, together with interference with rights of way, rights of light and other rights are all examples of "nuisance" under the Common Law which may give the person suffering from them a legal right of action. Also a question which is frequently asked is how far a homeowner may be responsible for the actions of his children or his, or their, animals. These questions are considered further in this chapter.

2. Noise, smells, smoke and fumes

There are many things which a homeowner may otherwise quite legitimately do upon his own land but which may give cause for complaint if they interfere with his neighbours' peaceful occupation of their properties. Actions which cause excessive or unreasonable noise or smells, or which produce offensive smoke or fumes are the most common. Such disturbance of the neighbours is called "nuisance" and may be the grounds for an action in the courts. A few examples of other actions which the courts have decided are a legal nuisance are:-

(a) Piling earth against the neighbour's wall which makes his house damp.

(b) Causing vibrations which damage his buildings.

(c) Using a building as a hospital for infectious diseases which causes the neighbours to live in constant fear of catching disease.

(d) Regularly watching or peering into a man's house.

(e) Causing excessive heat which makes his house too hot.

For some action, or state of affairs, to be a legal nuisance it must in general be continual for a long period, or constantly repeated. An occasional noisy party, or smoky bonfire, will not be grounds for a claim in the courts. On the other hand the regular shrieking of electric drills from a motor body repair yard, or the smell from pigsties, may be. However there are times when something which happens only occasionally, or even only once, is so serious that it may allow the neighbour who suffers to seek damages in the courts. This is particularly the case when the nuisance is of the kind which damages the neighbour's property or possessions. Examples of such a nuisance are causing vibrations which damage the structure of a neighbouring house, or allowing the escape of dangerous fumes which cause injury to the neighbour or damage his plants or animals.

The fact that noise, smell, or something equally unpleasant is coming from your neighbour's land does not necessarily mean that there are grounds for any kind of legal action. To begin with a person who buys or builds a house in an agricultural area next to a pig farm, or in an industrial zone next to a steel works, cannot complain about the smells or noise which come from them. It would be different if the pig breeder carried on his business in what was otherwise a residential area; he would then be at constant risk of being sued by one of his neighbours who objected to the smells. In most cases it is only when something happens to disturb what was previously a peaceful and enjoyable occupation of the property that something can be done about it. Then the question which has to be answered is: how bad an effect have the noises, smells etc had upon the neighbouring property or its owners?

It is in cases such as nuisance that one can see how appropriate it is for the scales to be the symbol of justice. The courts have to perform a balancing act weighing against each other the conflicting rights of the people involved. On the one hand is the right of A to have the freedom and liberty of using his land in a perfectly lawful manner, while on the other hand is the right of B to live in and enjoy his property in peace and free from disturbance. The result of this is that everyone can expect that from time to time his neighbour will do things that he dislikes, or which may even cause him extreme annoyance, but he will have to put up with them. It is no good for someone who is a light sleeper and whose sleep is regularly disturbed in the middle of the night by the family next door flushing their lavatory, which he can hear through the wall, to complain about it. Against this the man who likes to play grand opera at full blast on his hi-fi must accept that his neighbours are entitled to some peace and quiet and cannot be expected to suffer his entertainment too often or too late at night. There are few hard and fast rules, and the courts must consider each case which comes before them on its merits.

In striking the balance between the two neighbours the court will certainly take into account their motives. Although B may have to put up with a certain amount of noise from A's house, he can do something to stop it if A is making the noise to annoy him. This is well illustrated by the case of a music teacher whose next door neighbour got tired of hearing music lessons from the adjoining house. The neighbour began banging on the wall, beating on trays, whistling and shrieking. The court had no hesitation in ordering the neighbour to stop making the noises. However, if the noise made by the neighbour had been for some good reason, such as drilling or hammering the wall in the course of the construction of book shelves against it, rather than simply to annoy the music teacher, then almost certainly the court would have refused to act against him.

It is the law of nuisance which also applies to the interference with rights of way and other easements. An occasional interference such as blocking of a right of way by a parked vehicle will not give grounds for an action in the court. But if it happens regularly then the owner of the right may be able to obtain an injunction from the court ordering the car owner not to block the road again. On the other hand the person who has the benefit of the right of way may also be guilty of legal nuisance if he abuses the right by using it in an improper way. For example the owner of a right of way which passes across his neighbour's land and close to his neighbour's house, must not use it as a race track nor to allow him to peer through his neighbour's windows. Such an improper use may also make him a trespasser as is explained in Chapter 10.

Having established that some neighbouring owner is behaving in such a way as to be causing a legal nuisance, what then can you do about it? To begin with you can speak politely to the neighbour pointing out that what he is doing is disturbing you or even causing damage to your property. He may not even realise that he is upsetting you and is most likely to apologise and stop doing whatever it is. He may explain that it is something temporary which he has to finish but that it will soon be completed. But sometimes he will say that he intends to keep on with his activity, especially if it is something to do with a business from which he is earning his living. In that case you must decide whether the disturbance to your peace and quiet, or the damage, or possibility of damage, to your property is serious enough for you to go to law about it.

If you decide to go to law then you will, of course, seek legal advice about what action to take. The usual options are either direct action, as in the case of an obstructed right of way or a blocked drain, an action for damages, or an injunction. The possibility of direct action is generally best avoided and should only be resorted to in cases of the greatest urgency. The payment of compensation by way of damages is the only possible remedy in some cases, such as injury having been suffered by your house, but in most cases of continuing nuisance money is not adequate as a remedy. An injunction is the usual answer to the problem.

An injunction is an order of the court directing somebody to do something or, more commonly, not to do something. The order may be a positive one, as where it orders the neighbour to pull down the fence he has put up which blocks the light to your window, or prevents you driving your car down the private road to the back of your house. In most cases the injunction orders the neighbour to stop doing the thing complained of such as making excessive noise, or allowing offensive fumes to pour out of the chimney on his glue factory. The effect of the injunction is that someone who disobeys it is in contempt of court and may be sent to prison or fined heavily. In extreme cases the court may send its bailiffs to carry out the orders of the court themselves.

3. Trees

Other problems between neighbours falling under the heading of legal nuisance, can be caused by trees. They can interfere with light or air, overhang a neighbour's land or the highway, or push their roots under the neighbour's land causing damage in a variety of ways. There is yet another hazard, that their leaves or fruit may be poisonous to people or animals. As in the case of other nuisance the remedies for the neighbour who suffers are either an action for damages, an application to the court to grant an injunction, or, in the case of overhanging branches or encroaching roots in particular, self help.

Because of the slow rate of growth of most trees the question of what constitutes an interference to the right of light is even harder to decide than when the interference is man made. Undoubtedly growing trees can reduce the light to a window and eventually become intolerable. The problem for the homeowner whose light is blocked by a tree is to decide when it has become so bad that an application to the court is justified. He will, of course, first complain to the neighbour about the obstruction and request that the tree should be pruned, or, if necessary, removed altogether if it is seriously interfering with his light. If the tree, when it is first planted, should be put in a position close to a window, so that the light will inevitably be blocked out in time as the tree grows, it is advisable to point this out to the neighbour at once, suggesting that it should be moved to another position before it becomes really established. If the neighbour is reasonable he will no doubt see the validity of the complaint and take steps immediately to put matters right. However, if the neighbour will not do anything about it the homeowner may eventually have to go to law.

In that case the thing to do is to see a solicitor once the light becomes obstructed, and he will decide what evidence will be needed before the matter comes to court. As a first step he will write formally to the neighbour on your behalf demanding the immediate removal, or if appropriate the pruning, of the offending tree. If this does not produce results then he may have to commence proceedings.

Overhanging trees are obviously a more straightforward matter. When the branches of a tree project over your land there can be no doubt that there is an encroachment, and no question of having to satisfy a court that a nuisance exists. If necessary an order could be obtained to have the offending branches removed, but a much simpler remedy is to hand. It is well established that you may cut down overhanging branches at the point where they cross your boundary without having to obtain the permission of the neighbour on whose land the tree grows, or even to tell him that you intend to do it. There are, however, three important points to remember; you must not encroach on the neighbour's land in order to cut the branches; the wood and any fruit removed must be returned to the neighbour, assuming of course that he wants it; and you must take care to do as little damage as possible to the tree.

If trees, bushes, or hedges overhang the highway, whether it be a main road or a public footpath, causing an obstruction or some other nuisance, the local highway authority may take action to end the nuisance. They can, and often do, issue a formal notice requiring pruning of the offending trees or bushes. If a tree growing close to the road is old or decayed, and therefore dangerous, they can order that it be felled. If the landowner fails to carry out the work demanded, the highway authority can do it themselves then send him a bill for the cost of the work.

When the branches of a tree project over your land there can be no doubt that there is an encroachment.

Another case in which the highway authority may take action against a landowner is when he has a corner plot next to a road junction. A highway authority may declare that the corner of the plot must be kept clear of obstructions, including growing trees or plants, in order to provide a line of sight for traffic emerging from the side road, or turning into it. If the landowner permits trees or other plants to grow higher than a certain very limited height, usually only about one metre, then again the authority can order that they be removed, failing which they will remove them themselves and send him the bill.

Tree roots can be an even bigger hazard. The greatest problem is that they very frequently cannot be seen above ground, while some trees have very long roots indeed growing horizontally and close to the surface. These roots can find their way into the foundations of buildings or into drains. In either case they can cause considerable damage. Roots insinuating themselves into the brick foundations can weaken the structure by loosening the mortar between the bricks, or even splitting the individual bricks. But the greatest damage often occurs in times of drought when the trees suck out all the moisture from the ground around the building's foundations, allowing clay or certain other kinds of earth to crumble or crack so that the building subsides, sometimes causing irreparable harm.

Once more the homeowner whose land is invaded by roots from his neighbour's trees may take action of various kinds. If damage occurs to his buildings or drains he may claim compensation from the neighbour. Again he can cut through the roots at the point where they enter his land, or anywhere inside it. Indeed there may be a duty upon him, once he is aware of the encroaching roots, and the possibility of damage to his buildings, to take action to prevent the roots from reaching or damaging them. But as in the case of overhanging branches he must take care to do as little damage as possible to the tree, and he must certainly not do anything deliberately to harm the tree.

Finally there may be serious consequences of growing trees or plants near to a boundary which are poisonous to people or animals. Certainly a landowner has been held responsible for the death of a valuable horse which ate leaves from a yew tree, poisonous to horses, which grew near to his boundary and overhung the field in which his neighbour kept the horse. If this reasoning applies to yew trees and horses there may well be a similar liability for people, particularly children, or animals damaged by other poisonous trees or plants such as laburnum or the giant hog weed. If you wish to grow such plants upon your land it is advisable to keep them well away from your boundary fences or hedges.

4. Children, visitors and workmen

As a general rule parents are not responsible for the actions of their children. A child who is old enough to be sufficiently aware of what he or she is doing, and the effect which it will have, is treated in law as a responsible person in his or her own right. But when a child is too young to have this understanding then the parents must exercise control and may be responsible for harm or disturbance caused to other people by the child if they fail to do so.

When a parent is the occupier of property then this responsibility for the actions of other people can be extended to older children, and even adults. Note that it is the occupier of the property, not necessarily the owner, who must see that the neighbours are not disturbed, or they or their property injured, by some nuisance being committed on the land. He must therefore exercise reasonable control over people on his property, including members of his family or visitors to his property with his approval, and that includes people invited by other members of his family, or people who are taken to be there with his implied consent. If any such person does something which causes harm or nuisance to a neighbour, the occupier who has failed to exercise the control expected of him may himself be sued. However the occupier is not responsible for nuisance caused by a trespasser on his property when he does not know about it or is not able to control or prevent it.

If the occupier employs workmen to work on his property he may be responsible for nuisance caused by them. If the workmen are employees on the payroll of the occupier himself he is any case liable for whatever they do in the course of their employment. When the workmen are not on the payroll of the occupier, but are contractors brought in to do a particular job, then the occupier will not normally be liable to the neighbours if they do the job in a way which causes nuisance to the neighbours. But if the work which the contractors were engaged to do is itself the cause of the nuisance (e.g. when they are engaged to build a wall which blocks a right of way or obstructs the light to a neighbour's window) then obviously it is the occupier himself who is liable.

5. Dogs, cats and other animals

So far as the homeowner is concerned the animals which are most likely to be of interest to him are cats and dogs. They are sometimes the cause of disagreement between neighbours but there are special rules which apply to them. To begin with there can generally be no trespass by a dog or a cat. But if a dog, having strayed onto a neighbour's garden, attacks his animals, or the people who are there, the situation may be different.

There is a strict duty imposed on a dog owner to prevent it attacking livestock. A dog owner whose animal enters his neighbour's land and attacks his horse, cow, sheep or poultry is always liable to pay damages in compensation. Strangely enough the same strict duty does not apply if the dog attacks people or other dogs. In that case anyone wishing to make a claim against the owner or keeper of the dog must show that the owner or keeper knew that the dog was dangerous and likely to attack people or other dogs. However, a dog owner who deliberately sends his dog onto the land of another person will be liable for trespass and for any damage the dog causes.

Different rules apply to other animals. If your neighbour keeps other domestic animals (e.g. horses, cattle, sheep or goats), then he is responsible for any damage they may do to other property. Once again injury to people is not covered unless the owner or keeper of the animal knew it to be vicious. On the other hand when a wild animal is kept by someone, whether as a pet or in a cage, the owner will be responsible for any damage it does to people, animals, crops or property if it escapes.

There are of course other ways in which animals can be a source of trouble even without escaping from their owners. Smells and noise are frequently caused by animals and if either is excessive then the owner may be ordered to remove the animals. As in the case of other sources of smell or noise the rules about peaceful occupation apply, and the courts must balance the freedom of one person to keep animals against the freedom of his neighbours to enjoy occupation of their properties.

The flat dweller

1. Community living

The rapid increase in recent years in the number of flats and apartments in this country has presented both the law and the occupiers with new problems to be solved. Problems with neighbours over rights of way, noise, children, animals and a host of other sources of discontent are intensified by close proximity. The owner of a flat may have not just one or two neighbours separated from him by party walls, as in the case of a house owner, but possibly five, with one above, one below and one behind also. A flat dweller must therefore be both more tolerant of his neighbour's behaviour and more considerate of his neighbour's comfort than the average homeowner.

At one time such flats and apartments as existed were virtually all in tenement blocks in the big cities. Their occupiers were usually weekly tenants and if they found it intolerable to live there then they could move to another apartment or a rented house which were fairly easy to find in those days. But the last forty years have seen a development on a massive scale of blocks of flats by well meaning but misguided local authorities, who have filled them with tenants who never wished to live in a flat and who have had no means of escaping from this new and unwanted environment.

In tandem with this has been the development by private builders of blocks of flats for sale. The severe restrictions on land development imposed by the Town and Country Planning Acts has caused building land to be in increasingly short supply and consequently more expensive. The construction of blocks of flats to make maximum use of the land available has enabled builders to keep the prices down, and for many young people setting up home, or elderly people retiring, a flat has been the only kind of new home which they could afford. For these new flat owners, who have paid out their hard earned savings and/or committed themselves to repay expensive mortgages, it is essential that arrangements should be made wherever possible to ensure that their future occupation of the flats will be at least bearable.

The law of nuisance applies, of course, to the ownership and occupation of flats just as much as houses. However the system is rather cumbersome and is always subject to the interpretation of a particular judge as to the balance of the freedom of one occupier to do what he likes against the peaceful occupation by his neighbours. It is therefore usual to find that on the sale of flats the duties and obligations of each flat owner to his neighbours are set out in far more detail than is the case on the sale of a house. In most flat developments there are covenants given and regulations made setting out in detail what the occupier may or may not do. Such regulations frequently specify whether the occupier may keep pets in the flat, and if so what kind, where and when the occupier may hang out washing, when and how loudly he may play music or a radio, whether he may attach a window box to the outside of the flat, and so on. Anyone who would find such controls imposed upon him to be objectionable, should not consider buying or renting a flat.

2. Common parts and services

In addition to the psychological pressures which living in close proximity to large numbers of strangers can create, there are other practical difficulties to be overcome by flat dwellers. Because the flats are several home units grouped together within one building they share a common roof, common foundations, common drainage systems and a multitude of other things. It is not normally a practical solution to regard the whole building as physically divided into sections with one owner responsible for the condition of part of the roof while another must keep part of the foundations in repair. Either the flat owners must act together in unison as a community, or the control of the block of flats must be left in the hands of outsiders.

Regardless of the means adopted for the control and management of any particular block of flats the financial arrangements usually follow a fairly standard pattern. Each flat owner is called upon to pay, on a regular basis, a share of the cost of maintaining the block. The cost is divided between the flat owners on a percentage basis which may be equal shares for all, or unequal shares where certain flats are larger than others. The costs and expenses usually covered include such items as:-

1) The repair of the outside walls, roof and foundations of the building and also internal passages and staircases leading to the individual flats.
2) Cleaning and decorating those outside walls, roofs, staircases etc.
3) The repair of lifts: keeping them operational and safe.
4) Keeping the gardens in good repair and cared for by gardeners.
5) Providing lights and the supply of electricity to them for the outside of the building, inside passages and staircases etc.
6) Keeping the roads, footpaths, parking areas, main drains and sewers in good repair, and resurfacing or replacing them when necessary.

7) Sometimes providing central heating and hot water from a single heating plant.

In most cases the money to pay for all these common services is collected from the flat owners quarterly in advance. The person, company, or committee responsible for keeping the flats in repair will make an estimate at the start of each year of the likely cost of the services throughout the year and will demand payment of the appropriate proportion from each flat owner each quarter. At the end of the year proper accounts are prepared showing the exact cost of managing the flats and keeping them in repair. If the actual cost has been greater than the amount collected then the flat owners must each pay an additional sum. If the actual cost turned out to be less then the flat owners will each be given credit for the overpayment which will be knocked off the next year's payments, or alternatively the extra money will be held in an emergency fund to deal with unusually high expenses in the future when the roof needs replacing, or the internal roads must be relaid. The difficulties about such an arrangement arise in particular when one flat owner sells his flat, because he will wish to claim repayment of part of the emergency fund which means that a new owner will have to pay in an equivalent amount.

3. Freehold flats or leasehold flats?

Although one occasionally comes across a freehold flat, the vast majority of flats are leasehold. Some flats of course, are let to weekly or monthly tenants, others are let for relatively short terms subject to a rack rent, but an ever increasing number are let on long leases, usually for ninety-nine years subject to a ground rent.

Those flats which are sold with a freehold title are, on the whole, in large houses which have been converted to two or more self contained flats. When this occurs the owner of each flat is generally made responsible for the exterior parts of his premises. Where a house is divided between the ground floor and first floor the owner of the lower flat will be responsible for maintaining the foundations, and the upper flat owner will be responsible for the roof. One will covenant to provide adequate support for the flat above, while the other will covenant to protect the flat below from rain or other elements of the weather. In fact the law has never been very happy about the idea of such freehold flats. Because freehold ownership used to be regarded as synonymous with the ownership of land the law finds a "flying freehold" as it is called hard to swallow. How can the owner of a first floor flat be "land" owner when what he actually owns is the right for his buildings to hover in the air ten feet above the surface of the earth?

The main practical difficulty affecting freehold flats is the enforceability of the

The law finds a 'flying freehold' hard to swallow.

covenants. Because positive covenants will not pass with the property to a new owner on either side, there is a real problem for each flat owner every time any of the flats in the building are sold or, worse still, passes to a new owner on the death of the original owner. It is essential that each flat is protected by positive covenants made by the owners of all the other flats to provide that each of them will carry out such work as may be necessary to keep his property in repair for the sake of the safety and protection of the whole building. It is therefore advisable for every flat owner to join in the deed every time any flat changes hands so that the new owner of the flat, and the owners of all other flats in the building, enter new covenants with each other for their mutual benefit. Naturally this can present difficulties, especially if one flat owner is in dispute with his neighbours, or perhaps abroad on business at the relevant time. For all of these reasons building societies and other mortgagees are not usually prepared to lend money on a freehold flat or apartment.

Leasehold flats are a different proposition. The occupation by people, or businesses, of rooms or apartments in a building has long been known to the law and accepted as a proper commercial arrangement. The transition from short tenancies at a rack rent to long leases subject to a ground rent was easily made. The leasehold framework, in which there is a landlord owning the whole building with the leaseholder owning a part for a fixed period, is ideal for flat ownership. The covenants by each leasehold tenant can be enforced against him or against future owners of his flat by the landlord. At the same time the owner of each flat can force the landlord to carry out work himself or to ensure that it is carried out by the owner of some other flat to keep the building in repair for the benefit of all. An arrangement whereby the flat owners are each responsible for their own parts of the exterior of the building is very occasionally adopted, but the system outlined earlier where the landlord retains ownership of, and responsibility for, the outside of the building, the grounds, the common passages, and the staircases is more efficient and therefore is usually adopted.

A leasehold flat, therefore, is generally a better proposition for a purchaser than a freehold flat, although there are drawbacks. Because positive covenants can be enforced by the flat owner against his landlord, and _vice versa_, the flats can be more efficiently managed for the benefit of all. Building societies, banks and other mortgagees will be prepared to lend money on a leasehold flat which they would not lend if the flat were freehold, so it is more saleable. On the other hand the flat will remain leasehold with a limited life, the property will eventually revert to the landlord, and the value of the flat as a saleable asset will decline as the lease nears its end.

When the Leasehold Reform Act was passed giving leasehold owner occupiers the right to buy their freeholds (see page 23), flats were excluded. The reason for the exclusion is, of course, the very fact that a block of flats is more efficiently managed and controlled for the benefit of all the flat owners if the flats are leased. The exclusion it will be remembered also extends to houses where a substantial part lies under or over part of another building. Parliament decided, when the Act was passed, that the importance to such properties of the protection given by the positive covenants in a lease, outweighed the desirability for any individual owner to be allowed to buy his freehold. The only way for the owner of a leasehold flat to have a permanent and secure ownership is for him to own also a share in the freehold of the block of flats. Sometimes this happens, but regrettably for the tenants such an arrangement is all too rare.

4. The management of leasehold flats

Anyone considering buying a flat should seek information about the ownership and management of any which are being offered for sale. No doubt the principal concern of the prospective purchaser will be the accommodation, the situation, the outlook, and other physical characteristics of the flats which are on the market. He will also want to know the length of the lease, the amount of the ground rent and the average cost of the service charge. However he should also have in mind a number of factors which may affect the capital value, the annual cost, the convenience and the sheer pleasure of living in the flat of his choice. Some of these factors may turn out to be of greater importance than the physical characteristics, and in comparing the value of one flat against the value of another they may be very significant. Unfortunately a prospective purchaser will find that estate agents rarely have full information about established flats although for new flats it is in many cases readily available from the selling agents or the site office. Before deciding definitely that he wants to buy a particular flat, and especially if he should be making a choice between two or more flats in different blocks or developments, the would-be purchaser should insist on having all the relevant information. In particular he should find out who are the landlords, how is the block of flats managed, what are the covenants and regulations currently in force, and who is responsible for enforcing the observance of those covenants and regulations.

It is usually the landlord who is principally responsible for the management of the block of flats, or sometimes a larger complex containing several blocks. He may be the owner of the freehold or himself a leasehold owner if the block of flats itself is leasehold with underleases given to individual flat owners. Frequently the landlord is a company, which may be the builder company itself owning vast numbers of assets, or a small company created for the sole purpose of owning this block of flats. However the day to day management is most often in the hands of an estate agent who has been employed by the landlord or management company and whose fees are part of the expenses covered by the service charge imposed on each flat.

Many blocks of flats built within the last few years are managed by a separate management company. The builders or developers register a new company specifically to take over the management of the new property, and the leases of the flats impose on this company the duty of maintaining the common parts and services. The management company is also empowered to collect the service charges from the tenants of the flats, in order to cover the expenses. It may also be given authority to collect more than the actual expenses in any particular year and to hold any surplus monies at the end of each year in a special fund to cover extraordinary expenses which may crop up in future years. The good thing about this type of scheme from the point of view of the tenants is that each flat owner is normally given one share in the management company and the lease of each flat provides that when the flat is sold the share must also be transferred to the new owner. As the number of shares is usually equal to the number of flats, the management company is generally controlled by the tenants for the time being.

With a management company controlled by the flat owners themselves one really has democracy in action. They have an annual general meeting when they elect directors to manage the company. The directors can decide what expenses must be incurred and where money can be saved. Often they manage the flats themselves, so saving the expense of employing a managing agent. If the block of flats is a small one all the tenants can attend regular meetings to make the decisions, but in a big development the operation will be controlled by their elected committee, the board of directors of the management company. In such a scheme the freehold landlord collects the ground rents but the management company levies the service charges. If either the landlord or any of the tenants is unhappy about the way the flats are being managed he can force the management company to carry out its duties properly under the covenants which it has given to all the other parties.

A management company controlled by the tenants is good for the tenants but much better is a special landlord company controlled by the tenants. Sometimes the builder or developer creates a new company similar to a management company then transfers to it the freehold of the flats. Each flat owner then purchases a share in the landlord company so that when all the flats are sold the tenants are also joint owners of the freehold through the company. This is the ideal arrangement for a flat owner. The ground rent paid by each tenant goes into the same fund as the service charge. The company has no obligation to an outside landlord but is wholly responsible to the tenants themselves. Best of all the flats revert to the company landlord at the end of the leases but the tenants do not lose them. They can grant new leases to themselves. Anyone owning a flat within such a scheme has an asset worth more than most flats.

Whatever the arrangements for management of the flats may be, it is important that full and accurate accounts are kept. If the landlord manages the flats, either directly or through an agent, the tenants will need to be shown details of the expenses incurred each year and the income from the service charges which covers the payments. Such accounts should be properly audited with the receipts for the payment examined against the books of account just as would be done for any private business. In most cases the lease of each flat will direct that copies of audited accounts should be given to the tenant each year, but in any case a tenant who has not received such accounts within a reasonable time of the end of the accounting year should insist on their production by the landlord. It is especially important that the accounts should show how any surplus is dealt with when the service charges exceed the expenses. If the surplus is retained to cover future expenses it should be properly invested and the interest from such investment also paid into the reserve fund.

Where the tenants themselves manage the flats through a management company or by owning the landlord company it is equally important that records are kept and proper accounts prepared each year. Again the company must be run as though it were a business even though the tenants own it themselves and it exists only for the benefit of their occupation of the flats. Each year the company must make returns to the Companies Registry and also tax returns. If interest is earned on any monies held in reserve, or even on current balances during the year, Corporation Tax will be payable. It is very easy for such things to be overlooked especially if the company, which is not an ordinary trading company anyway, is being run by tenants or a tenants' committee who are not used to running a private company or a business. From the very beginning proper account books must be kept and entries made of all money paid to or by the company. Receipts should be obtained for all payments and at the end of the year the accounts should be prepared, audited, and copies given to each tenant.

Extensions, alterations, improvements and other development

1. Planning consent and Building Regulation approval

Most homeowners are well aware of the requirement to get planning permission before beginning building work. They have probably also heard that certain small extensions can be carried out without planning consent. However they may not always realise that there are other consents necessary under the London Building Acts for property in London, or under the local building bye-laws for property in other parts of the country; and that planning consent may be necessary for other work or alterations to the property, or the way in which it is used.

Since the Town and Country Planning Act 1947 came into force, no-one has been allowed to put up a building in this country without first obtaining planning consent. There are basically two kinds of planning consent, outline planning consent when the proposal for a particular development is approved in principle, and detailed planning consent when the detailed plans of the building to be erected are approved. Even when the detailed consent is given the planning authority may make the consent conditional on further detailed information being supplied and approved. The average homeowner will not be interested in outline permission because he will be wishing to apply for consent to build an extension onto his house or put up a garage or some other outbuilding, so he will simply apply for detailed consent submitting plans and architect's drawings showing exactly what building or alteration he wishes to make. But sometimes a homeowner may want outline consent when he is considering the possibility of turning part of his garden into a site for another house, converting his house into flats, or starting some business there.

A useful first step is to contact the planning department of the local planning authority and make an appointment to see the planning officer who deals with the district in question. The local planning authority is usually the District Council. Planning officers are professional planners employed by the local authority to advise the council about planning matters, and although they do not themselves make the actual planning decisions, their views carry a lot of weight. Whether a particular proposal is to be approved or rejected is decided by local councillors on the planning committee and their decision is later ratified at a meeting of the Council. Although the committee can reject the planning officer's advice about a particular application, they will frequently be guided by what he thinks about it. Therefore a discussion with him right at the beginning can give a very good indication as to whether a particular proposal is likely to be acceptable, and the local planning officer is often very helpful to the applicant who may have several different schemes in mind.

Having decided upon the proposals he intends to make, the applicant must obtain planning application forms from the Council. He also obtains from them building regulations application forms. Both applications are completed, detailed plans and drawings are prepared, and they are all sent to the Council. The Council will send a notice to each of the neighbouring owners giving brief details of the application which has been made and the neighbours are invited to inform the Council of any objections they may have to the proposals. A notice is also placed in a local newspaper to give the general public information about the proposed development, and again anyone who dislikes it may lodge an objection with the Council.

Eventually the Planning Committee of the Council will consider the application and either approve it or reject it. The Committee will consider all the objections which have been raised as well as the advice given by the planning officers but it is the Committee members who will make the decision. If the Council rejects the proposals the applicant may appeal against their decision to the Secretary of State for the Environment. Alternatively he can always make a new application for something different, which may in fact contain only minor variations from his original application.

On the other hand the application may be approved, in which case that is the end of the matter, except that the Council may direct that additional information is to be given, or may make the planning consent subject to other conditions which have to be complied with. If an outline planning application is approved then the consent given will be outline consent, and the applicant must submit his detailed plans and provide any additional information required by the Council within three years. Once a full planning consent has been given the work must be commenced within five years.

There are occasions when a person begins work on his property without first obtaining the necessary planning consent. If that happens he may be fined and also ordered to return the property to its original state. The situation is the same if, having obtained planning permission, he carries out work which is not in accordance with the consent given. However the Council cannot take any action against him unless they do so within four years of the work being completed.

If an owner makes a change in the use of his property for which he has not obtained the necessary consent, he can again be fined and will probably be ordered to return the property to its original use. In that case the Council has the power to enforce the change back to the original use of the property even though the unauthorised change took place more than four years earlier.

Whenever it is discovered by the Council that a change of use has taken place it can make an order that the new use should stop, even after many years. However, the Council's powers can be used in this way only if the change of use has taken place since 1964. Before that date the same rules applied to a change of use as apply to building work, so the Council had to take action within four years of the change.

2. Building works which require planning permission

Any new building must be approved by the planning authority before it is erected. Where an existing building is extended, knocked down and rebuilt, or in some cases simply altered in appearance, planning consent is necessary. Other structures which are not buildings at all may be subject to planning consent, such as fences around gardens, car ports, flagpoles etc. Works on the ground may also be subject to the planning laws, and of particular interest to the homeowner is the restriction on making or widening an access to the highway. There are however certain exemptions which relieve him of the need to obtain planning consent in particular cases, some of which apply particularly to private houses.

Unless it falls within one of the exemptions any enlargement of any existing house will need planning approval. The main exemption is that there is no need to obtain planning permission for an extension which does not add more than either 50 cubic metres or 10% of the existing building (with a maximum of 115 cubic metres) whichever is greater. The outside of the extension is measured so it will include any roof space and the thickness of the walls. However the extension must not increase the height of the original house and it must not extend towards the road at the front of the house. On the other hand, the exemption does apply to the building of a garage, stable or loose box if the size is within the 50 cubic metres or 10%. Also the conversion of a room into a garage or *vice versa* is covered by the exemptions and does not require planning permission.

If an extension is built, adding to the total size of the house, it is the original size of the house which is the basis for calculating the size of the addition. Either the house will have been standing since before the present town and country planning law came into operation in 1948, or it was built in accordance with planning permission given since then. Each addition built on to the house is measured against the size of the house as it stood in 1947, or the house built in accordance with the full planning permission since then. Once an extension has been made, a further enlargement of the house is not permitted if it takes the increase in size above the limit of 50 cubic metres or 10% of the *original* house. This is so even when the first alteration was made with full planning consent.

The second kind of permitted alteration to an existing house is the building of a porch outside a door. The floor area of such a porch must not exceed two square metres, and it must be no higher than three metres above ground level. In addition there must be at least two metres between the porch and the boundary of the highway. The big difference between this exemption applying to porches and the general exemption for small extensions is that the porch may extend the house towards the road. No other extension towards the road is allowed without specific planning permission being granted. Even the addition of a brick cladding or stone facing to the front of a house cannot be made without planning permission because it extends the house towards the road.

Apart from these alterations to a house, including a garage, stable or loose box, certain other small buildings may be put up without consent being obtained. These are described as any building or enclosure "for a purpose incidental to the enjoyment of the dwelling-house". They include such things as a greenhouse, garden shed, dog kennel, bee hive or poultry shed, but not a garage or stable. No part of such a building must be nearer the road than is the front of the house and it must not exceed three metres in height, or four metres if it has a ridged roof. The total ground area covered by such outbuildings must not exceed half of the garden land. Also it is important that it should be connected with the enjoyment of the house and only for the benefit of the occupants. A hen house in which a dozen hens will live, laying eggs which are mainly eaten by the family, is acceptable, but a large battery hen house is not.

A further exemption which applies just to private houses is for an oil tank containing central heating oil. The tank must not exceed 3,500 litres in capacity and must be no higher than three metres from ground level. Again it must not project beyond the front of the house towards the road.

There is no restriction on keeping a private car in the drive or garden of a house. In fact several cars belonging to members of the household may be kept there and can be repaired there without causing any breach of the planning laws. Visitors' cars parked there from time to time are permissible but the homeowner must not begin to use his garden as a car park for other people. He cannot carry on a business by charging people to leave their cars on his land, but he could let his garage to a neighbour who can keep a car in it. A small van or other small commercial vehicle may be kept at a house but a large lorry, or several commercial vehicles, could not be kept there without planning approval.

Similarly a caravan belonging to the homeowner may be kept in his garden but he cannot use the garden as a caravan site. The caravan may be kept there for storage between holidays, and may be slept in by members of the household. However the homeowner cannot allow someone who is not a member of the household to occupy a caravan on his land whether it is his own or the other person's.

Another restriction which is of major importance to the homeowner prevents the construction of an entrance from the road. Although it is certainly not a building an access to the highway is caught under the classification of an engineering operation. With the exception of an access to certain unclassified roads, no new access way can be constructed nor an existing access widened without planning permission. This restriction applies to an entrance for pedestrians as well as one designed for cars. It applies to widening an existing entrance as well as constructing a new one altogether. Even making a gap in a hedge through which a person may walk is regarded as constructing an access. Also the removal of a low wall or fence separating a garden from the highway is prohibited because it increases the access.

3. Change of use

In addition to controlling building works the Town and Country Planning Acts regulate any change in the use of land and buildings. The controls on erecting buildings affect both the use and the appearance of an area but the limitations placed on changing the use of property can be just as important in terms of the preservation of the environment and the enjoyment of life of the people who live there.

It will be noticed that the laws prevent changes in the use of land rather than imposing a total control on its use. An existing use of a particular property which has been carried on since before 1948 cannot be stopped now unless it is actually illegal or prohibited by some Act of Parliament. It does not matter that an existing use is one which is alien to the area where it is carried on such as a pig farm in an expensive residential area or a scrap metal merchant's yard in an area of natural beauty. Of course no-one in such a position is likely to be given permission to begin using their land for such a business now, but because it is the existing use the planning laws cannot alter it.

To the homeowner, the most important aspect of the planning laws is the restriction on erecting or extending buildings, but he must also remember that the rules about change of use may well affect some of the things he may consider doing in or to his house. The first thing he should note is that a single house cannot be turned into two or more flats, apartments or even semi-detached houses without planning consent. He may be surprised to learn, however, that where a house is already converted into flats he may re-convert it into a single house without obtaining any planning permission. It is always the increase in the number of living "units" which is restricted, so where planning consent has been given for a large house to be divided into four flats they cannot be further divided to make six flats, although they could be altered to make them into just three flats. Also the restriction is on the conversion of the building to make separate dwelling units, so the sharing of the house or the taking in of a lodger will not normally be a change of use for which planning approval will be needed.

A family or "family group" may share a house or flat without creating any change of use for planning purposes. A group of friends buying or renting a house between them, sharing the kitchen, the bathroom, and perhaps the dining room or lounge, will still be using it as a single dwelling-house. Also a family may take in an au pair, a maid, or a lodger or two, but just where the line should be drawn can be very difficult to decide. If a house is used as a hotel, a guest house, or a boarding house then the owner is carrying on a business and needs planning permission for a change of use. If the house is converted into bed sitting rooms let to individual tenants then, even though they have joint use of the kitchen and bathroom, there is a change of use into what is known as "multiple paying occupation" and again planning permission must be obtained. But at what point can it be said that a family taking in lodgers has ceased to be a family group occupying the house as a single unit, and has become either a boarding house or a property in multiple paying occupation? In a borderline case only the court can decide whether the house is still used as a single private dwelling-house, after considering all the relevant facts of that particular case.

It is obvious that there is a change of use if a house is converted into a block of offices or a school. It is not so obvious when part of the house, or the outbuildings, or the garden, is used for some different purpose, and especially if that part is used for a business of some kind. When there is a "material change of use" of part of the property then again planning permission will be required but once again it can be very difficult to draw the line. Generally speaking the use of part of the property for some hobby or leisure activity will not be a change of use, nor will an occasional or "insignificant" use. However there are times when the leisure activity becomes a business, or the occasional use becomes too frequent. These are discussed further in Chapter 13.

4. Building byelaw regulations and the London Building Acts

Far older than the planning laws are the London Building Acts, for property in Greater London; and the Building Regulations in other parts of the country. These were introduced to make sure that the buildings which are put up are soundly built and do not present any hazard to health or safety. They relate to such matters as methods of construction, the building materials used, fire

Building regulations apply when a building not previously used for human habitation is converted into a house.

precautions, lighting, ventilation, sanitary arrangements and drainage. In some cases they also relate to changes in use, particularly when a house is converted into two or more dwellings, or a building not previously used for human occupation is converted into a house.

Consent under the provisions is required quite separately from, and in addition to, consent under the Town & Country Planning Acts, and must be obtained before any building work commences. It is also necessary for alterations which are not affected by the planning laws. When alterations are proposed for which no planning consent is needed, because either they are internal, such as the removal of an internal wall, or they come within one of the exemptions, such as a small extension of less than fifty cubic metres, an application must still be made for consent under the building regulations or London Building Acts. As in the case of planning consent, an application is made on forms which are obtained from the local authority. In addition to the written information about the work which is to be carried out, the applicant must supply detailed plans and drawings similar to those which have to accompany planning applications.

It is not uncommon for work which requires this type of consent to be done without anyone applying for the consent first. In such a case the council can impose a fine on the owner and can also force him to undo the work unless he makes a proper application and files plans and drawings which are acceptable. In general the Councils' powers of enforcement are restricted to one year from the completion of the work for simple physical alterations to the buildings, but there are certain cases in which a Council can take action at any time where health or safety are at risk. For example a building may be dangerous either because the structure is overloaded or the building is dilapidated, or there may be a risk to health caused by insanitary conditions.

5. Restrictions in the deeds

Almost all leasehold properties, and a high proportion of freehold properties, are affected by covenants restricting the use of the property or the erection or alteration of buildings. Before the days of town and country planning restrictions the owner of a piece of land could do more or less what he liked with it. Houses or flats could be built, a factory could be erected, or it could be turned into a scrap yard. Restrictions for particular places were introduced from time to time, such as those relating to National Parks, but the only general protection for the environment was the law of nuisance (as mentioned in Chapter 6). Landowners who sold pieces of their land therefore considered it most important that the purchasers should be restrained from using that land in a manner which would be offensive, and made them covenant not to use it in certain ways. Builders who developed housing estates, being equally concerned about maintaining a controlled environment for the people who would buy and live in the houses, regularly imposed covenants that prevented the purchasers from using the houses for particular offensive businesses, or frequently for any business use except one or two named professions such as that of a doctor or lawyer.

Although there are today tight controls on development under the Town and Country Planning Acts, the restrictions in the deeds are still operative. One might have expected the modern planning laws to have made restrictions in the deeds more or less obsolete, and the imposition of new restrictive covenants a rarity, but this is far from the case. Upon the sale of a house on a new housing estate the purchaser nearly always has to enter into new covenants, and in many ways they are often more restrictive nowadays than those which were regularly imposed a hundred years ago. Such covenants usually prevent the house from being used for business purposes and often state that the homeowner will not put up new buildings or alter the existing ones without consent.

It is important that the homeowner should not overlook the effect of restrictive covenants when he is considering making any change to his property. He may obtain planning consent and building byelaw consent to build an extension to his house, but could still be prevented by someone who has the benefit of a covenant against building. Even the construction of a garden shed or greenhouse which requires no planning consent, and for which consent under the building regulations is a mere formality, may be a breach of the restrictive covenants. Similarly the fact that he has obtained planning consent to convert his house into flats, or to use it as a guest house, will not protect him from any action by someone who has the benefit of a covenant prohibiting such uses. Before embarking on any such schemes the homeowner should check what restrictions are in his deeds and, if necessary, apply for consent under the covenant or for release of the particular covenant.

As mentioned in Chapter 3, the difficulty sometimes is in discovering just who should give the consent required, or grant the release from the covenant. In the case of covenants contained in a lease it is easy to see who to approach because the homeowner will be paying ground rent to his immediate landlord, who will usually be the person entitled to enforce the covenant. However in the case of freeholds the covenant will be attached to another piece of land and may by now exist for the benefit of several neighbouring owners who have each bought a part of that land. In the case of a building scheme, where the covenants on each plot of a building estate are identical and each exist for the benefit of all the other householders on the estate, the situation is worse still. Even the leasehold owner may have added difficulty because these covenants may have originated on the grant of a headlease, passed on to him when an underlease was granted. Indeed they may have been created originally on a sale of the freehold, and passed on to him later when the lease was granted. What then should the homeowner do about it?

Where possible he should discover exactly who are the people entitled to enforce the covenant, and obtain consent or a release from each of them. If he cannot discover who can enforce the covenant then he may make an application to the court to be released from the covenant. This is usually applicable in the case of his wishing to convert the house into flats or offices or to some other use, when the court will release the covenant if the nature of the district has changed so much that the covenant becomes irrelevant. The problems are discussed further on pages 128 to 131, but in any case like this it is advisable to consult a solicitor.

Alternatively the homeowner may simply ignore the existence of the covenant and carry on with his proposals anyway. In practice this very often happens, particularly where the proposal is something fairly innocuous like putting up a garden shed or small greenhouse. The chances are that no-one will ever object anyway and the longer it goes without a challenge being made the harder a neighbour would find it to make a successful challenge. However the homeowner who begins any building alteration or change of use without release from the covenant is always taking a risk that some neighbour may immediately lodge an objection which will prevent him from doing what he wished, or at the best, will cause him serious delay. Worse than that is the possibility that he may be forced at a later date to pull down the building or extension which he has built. Even if no challenge is made at the time he may well experience difficulty when he comes to sell his property if he cannot prove to the purchaser that he did obtain all necessary consents first.

6. Planning applications by other people

There are two ways in which a homeowner may be affected by someone else making a planning application. The first is when a neighbour applies for a planning consent to build or to change the use of his property. The second is when somebody makes an application for planning consent to develop land including the homeowner's own property or part of it.

It is, of course, the application by a neighbour proposing to develop his own property which is by far the more common. Most owners are likely to learn at some time during their ownership that someone plans to put up a building on a neighbouring site, or extend his house, or convert it into flats or offices. The information may come direct from the Council, giving notice of intended developments to owners with adjoining properties, or may be seen in a local newspaper where planning proposals are advertised. If he dislikes the proposals the homeowner may write to the Council stating his reasons for objecting to the intended development. A simple statement that he does not like the proposal will not carry much weight with the Council but there is usually some sound reason for his dislike such as the fact that a proposed building will block his light or his view or will be an eyesore. If the proposal is to build commercial buildings or convert a home into offices or flats then a declaration that this will have a bad effect on the area, especially if it is a residential area, will often be a valid reason for opposing it.

The second type of planning application which someone else may make and which may seriously concern the homeowner is a proposal affecting his own land. Usually in such a case he will be well aware of it because the applicant will be a proposed purchaser who wants to alter the property or change its use. Very often in such a case the intended sale of the property will be conditional upon the purchaser getting the consent he wants so the homeowner will certainly not wish to oppose it. However there are occasions when an application may be made about which the owner knows nothing. This can occur when a neighbouring owner or even a complete outsider, has ideas of carrying out some scheme which will only be viable if the homeowner's land, or part of it, is included in the planning consent. Anyone wishing to carry out any development including someone else's property must deliver to them copies of all the plans and proposals he sends to the Council. The homeowner receiving notice of an application like this may well object strongly to anyone applying for consent affecting his land, but it may be worth his enquiring further into it before delivering a written objection. The proposed scheme may perhaps be for the building of a shopping centre or some other expensive development which if approved could make his property worth much more as a piece of building land than it is as a house and garden.

7. Listed buildings and ancient monuments

Certain buildings and other structures which are of special historic or architectural interest are recorded in a list kept by the Secretary of State for the Environment. They are referred to simply as listed buildings. All surviving buildings erected before 1700 which are in anything like their original condition are included in the list. Most surviving buildings which were put up between 1700 and 1840 are also on the list. There are quite a few buildings which were built after 1840 included on the list, but only those of real quality are considered as suitable. As yet there are very few included which were constructed after 1914.

The list separates the buildings into three categories indicating their relative importance. They are as follows:-

I Buildings of exceptional interest.

II*Buildings of particular importance and perhaps containing outstanding features.

II Buildings of special interest which warrant every effort being made to preserve them.

Ancient monuments are even more carefully preserved and protected than listed buildings. They are referred to as Scheduled Monuments and a schedule of these monuments is also kept by the Secretary of State in which the details of each are recorded. If a house is old enough, and of sufficient historical significance, it may be both a listed building and a scheduled monument. Furthermore scheduled monuments may be areas of land on which no building is now standing, but beneath which there is a known structure of historic importance.

The effect of any building, structure, or area of land, being a listed building or scheduled monument, is that much tighter control is kept on any proposed development, demolition, or alteration. The owner who wishes to carry out any development which requires planning consent must still obtain the normal planning consents and building byelaw consents, but he must first obtain the special Listed Building Consent from the local planning authority, or the even more exclusive Scheduled Monument Consent which can be given only by the

Secretary of State. In the case of a property which is both a listed building and a scheduled monument it is the Scheduled Monument Consent which has to be obtained. What he must always remember is that he cannot demolish the building or structure, and must not do anything else which will in any way alter or damage it, without first obtaining the appropriate special consent. The fact that ordinary planning consent would not have been required for the work he proposes to do is irrelevant, and he is likely to be prosecuted if he damages the property, or even makes a small change in it, unless he has obtained the necessary consent.

Once a building has become a listed building, or scheduled monument, the restrictions affect all buildings within the "curtilage" of the main building. In practice this usually means all outbuildings and other structures within the group of buildings which might be around a courtyard, in the garden, or generally within the area which is enclosed by walls, fences or hedges around the main building. It can also include the walls or fences themselves, and the gates. Whenever the owner of a listed building intends to do anything which might affect the appearance he should make enquiries to see whether Listed Building Consent might be needed.

In addition to particular buildings being listed, there are sometimes whole villages or other areas which are designated as conservation areas. Once an area has been made into a conservation area the buildings within it are all controlled in a similar way to listed buildings. Anyone owning a house or other property within a conservation area should make enquiries about what consents may be needed before beginning any work upon it.

The owner of a listed building or scheduled monument is required to keep it in a good state of repair. Although he is in fact the owner of the building, he is regarded as its custodian whose duty it is to preserve part of the nation's heritage. If he neglects it the local Council may send him a notice telling him what repairs are needed, and he must carry them out. If he fails to do this the Council may carry out the work themselves, then send the owner the bill for payment. In the past it was not uncommon for an owner to neglect a property so that it became unsafe, which gave him a valid reason for pulling it down. If a Council feel that an owner may be deliberately neglecting his property, they now have the power to compulsorily purchase it so that they can then put it into repair themselves.

On the brighter side for the owner of a listed building is the fact that grants are often available to assist him to pay for major repairs. There are grants which an owner can obtain for certain improvements and repairs to old buildings, as mentioned in the next part of this chapter, whether such old buildings are listed buildings or not. In addition there are special grants available to the owners of listed buildings, but they are usually limited to 25% of the cost. Sometimes extra money may be obtained from one of a number of bodies interested in preserving the heritage of the nation, such as the Historic Buildings and Monuments Commission. It is certainly worth making enquiries about what grants may be available before embarking on any repair work.

8. Home improvement grants

There are a number of cases in which the owner of a house or flat may obtain money from his local Council to pay for, or as a contribution towards, the cost of improving or repairing his home. The money given is called a home improvement grant. In a certain limited number of cases the owner is entitled to the grant if he can show that the property lacks certain basic amenities which are regarded as essential features of any new home. In all the other cases the grants may be given at the discretion of the local authority provided that the proposed improvements or alterations fall within one of the particular categories.

The grants available for basic amenities are called intermediate grants. The things they cover are a toilet (normally inside the dwelling), an inside bath or shower (usually in a bathroom), a wash hand basin, a sink, and a hot and cold water supply. There is a fixed limit of grant available for each of these improvements, and further information about them can be obtained from your local Council.

The only drawback about obtaining a grant for these basic improvements is that the Council can insist that the house or flat be put into condition "fit for human habitation" once the work covered by this intermediate grant is completed. The cost to the homeowner of doing this may be considerably higher than the amount of the grant received. However it is possible to make a claim for a smaller amount for minor repairs which will enable the basic amenities to be installed without the Council insisting on further work to bring the property up to a fully acceptable standard.

It is probably better, in most cases where work is required for the installation of basic amenities, to apply for a full improvement grant, provided that the property comes within the limits of those eligible for a full grant. It applies to older houses which have a rateable value of not more than £400 in Greater London or £225 elsewhere in the country. The grant can be obtained by the owner of a house or flat which is generally below the standard of a house regarded as being fit for human habitation. It is the Council which can decide whether a grant will be made available in any particular case, but provided that a grant is given it can cover many other improvements, and also a substantial contribution towards major structural repairs as well as the very basic necessities which would be covered by an intermediate grant.

In addition to giving grants for bringing a house or flat up to standard the local authorities are empowered to give an improvement grant to someone who wishes to convert a house into two or more flats. If the owner is to live in one of the flats himself, he must intend to let the other flat, or flats, when the conversion has been completed. In the case of a conversion of a house into flats the rateable value of the original house has to be not more than £600 if it is in Greater London, or £350 elsewhere, for it to qualify for an improvement grant of this kind.

The third category of grant is a repairs grant, available only to owners of properties built before 1919 which are in need of major structural repairs. This kind of grant is again limited to properties with a rateable value not exceeding £400 in London and £225 elsewhere. Once more it is given at the discretion of the Council. The difference between a repairs grant and an improvement grant is that in a repairs grant case the owner may be intending to do repairs only. Although some major structural repairs are sometimes covered by an improvement grant, the main purpose of that kind of grant is an improvement in the amenities or quality of the building, and only part of such a grant can be allowed towards putting the original property back into a good state of repair.

Fourthly there is a special form of grant available to the owner of a property in multiple occupation. This grant is for basic improvements and for the installation of a fire escape. It applies to houses which are occupied by lodgers or by tenants who share facilities. In properties converted to self contained flats any work to improve facilities will be covered by the ordinary improvement grant. Once again these grants are given at the discretion of the Council.

In the cases of all these grants there are strict limits imposed upon the total amount which can be given for any property. Also the Council is not obliged to pay to the owner the whole cost of doing the improvements or repairs, and may decide, in any particular case where it has discretion, that a proportion only of the cost will be met by the Council. In the vast majority of all cases where grants are given, part of the cost has to be met by the owner himself. However it is usual for the Council concerned to make further money available to the owner in the form of a loan repayable by instalments and secured by a mortgage on the property. Anyone applying for a grant who will have difficulty in raising the balance of the money to do the work, including any further work to bring the house to a proper standard of fitness for habitation which the Council may require, should enquire about the possibility of a loan from the Council, or from his building society or other mortgagee, before he applies for the grant. In the case of the monies provided under any such loan being used for an actual improvement in the property, then tax relief will be available on the mortgage interest payments if the money is borrowed at the time when the work has to be paid for. A loan borrowed at a later date is unlikely to benefit from this tax relief as is mentioned in Chapter 10.

At the present time there is yet another type of grant available to the homeowner. It is for the installation of roof insulation and cavity wall insulation in houses. It was introduced by the Government to save fuel on a national basis by preventing heat loss from residential property. These grants are also administered in each area by the local Council who will give you further information on request.

If you own a house which may qualify for a grant and wish to carry out improvements, the best course is to contact the Planning Department at your local Council. One of the Planning Officers will usually be pleased to discuss the problems with you, to advise you about what grants might be available, and to give you the appropriate forms for making an application.

Compulsory purchase and other powers of public bodies

1. Compulsory purchase in general

In the years since the Second World War vast areas of land in Great Britain have been compulsorily purchased. Under the powers given to them by the Housing Acts, local authorities have the right to make whole areas of houses into clearance areas or redevelopment areas. A clearance area is described as an area of slum property which is unfit for human habitation and which is incapable of being rendered fit for habitation at a reasonable cost. A redevelopment area is an area which is said to be in need of redevelopment because it is overcrowded or unfit. In an excess of zeal local councils throughout the country used these powers to the full in order to demolish old houses by the hundred thousand, particularly in the larger cities where mile after mile of inner city areas were laid waste.

At first there were many old terraced and back to back houses which really did need demolishing. Many of the inner cities had suffered badly from the German blitz, houses being knocked down or burnt out by the bombs. There were houses boarded up with bulging walls and sagging roofs which were a danger to the public. Even the houses which had escaped bomb damage and were still occupied had suffered from the lack of resources to keep them in repair during six years of war. With their leaking roofs and porous walls they were so riddled with damp and rot that they genuinely were unfit for human beings to live in. Unfortunately once having got a taste for demolition many local councils seemed to become insatiable. Having compulsorily purchased and demolished the thoroughly bad houses they turned their attention to those which were not quite so bad, and, when they in turn had been pulled down, to houses and housing areas which were certainly not in the same unfit category as those on which they had started. There were times when one could stand in an inner city area looking across miles of desolation with only the occasional public house still standing in the wasteland which otherwise might have been the aftermath of some nuclear war.

In those early days there were many people whose houses were taken from them for what amounted to peanuts. The regulations which governed the calculation of compensation to be paid to the owners were grossly unfair. If a house was declared unfit for habitation then the owner was not entitled to any payment for the building, and would be paid site value only. Furthermore the regulations provided that in assessing the value of the site of a house no account could be taken of the fact that adjoining plots were also being bought by the Council. Because the building regulations, which contained requirements such as that any new house built on the site must be set back from the road, and must have air space at the back of the house, usually prevented a new house from being built on the site, houses with small sites were almost worthless.

The former occupiers, whether they had been owner-occupiers or tenants with protected tenancies, were moved, often with great reluctance, into the tower blocks of flats or great barrack like apartment buildings which the councils in their wisdom built to replace the houses they demolished. A high proportion of these new developments, as everyone now knows, very rapidly became the slums of the later twentieth century. In some ways they were, from the beginning, less fit for human habitation than the terraced houses they had replaced. As the public began to realise this a general outcry arose against the policies which had led to the building of them. Coupled with this came more humane regulations which entitled people to receive more realistic compensation for their houses and prevented the councils from acquiring valuable building land for next to nothing. The result was the end of the age of large scale compulsory purchase. Homeowners were encouraged instead to improve their sub-standard houses and with the help of grants and loans to bring them into an acceptable state of fitness for habitation.

There are still of course, houses which the local authorities purchase because they are unfit, but the majority of compulsory acquisitions are now for other reasons. In an organised society it is inevitable that land, which sometimes includes private houses, will be required for public uses of many kinds. Land has to be bought for new roads, or to widen and improve existing roads. New towns are planned and the New Town Corporation buys large areas on which to build them. Airports, railway stations, military camps, reservoirs, power stations, and now the Channel Tunnel all need land, and it is acquired under the powers of compulsory purchase. However it is not always the local councils who exercise the right to buy the land. Other bodies such as British Rail, the Water Boards, the Central Electricity Generating Board, the Ministry of Defence, or any one of a host of Government departments and public bodies have, or may be given, compulsory purchase powers so that they can buy the land they need for their operations.

2. Compulsory purchase procedures

One of the problems for any property owner affected by a compulsory purchase order is that the development scheme which makes the purchase of his land necessary may well have been decided before he receives any formal and direct notice of it. The local council may have designated an area as an industrial zone, the highway authority may have decided to widen a road, the Secretary of State for the Environment may have decided upon the position of a new motorway, or the Water Board may have decided to flood a valley to create a new reservoir. Once these decisions have been made the purchase of the land to allow them to proceed becomes essential. At that point the owner receives a notice of the intended compulsory purchase which is the first direct communication to be addressed to him. Already it is too late for him to object because his continued occupation of his house in the middle of a motorway or at the bottom of a lake is out of the question. All he can do now is to negotiate on the terms for compensation.

Fortunately any proposals by the local authority or other public body for any such scheme must be duly advertised before the final decision is made. This gives the owner whose property may be affected the opportunity to lodge an objection. The advertisements appear in the London Gazette and a local newspaper; sometimes notices are also posted up on the land itself. Generally where any major project is under consideration, such as the building of a new airport or the construction of a motorway, there is considerable publicity and public debate so that it would be hard for anyone to avoid hearing about it. Unfortunately there is a time limit set for anyone to lodge an objection which is usually six weeks from the date of the publication of the proposals, six weeks being the minimum time which must be allowed. It is therefore, important for anyone hearing of proposals which will affect his property, either directly or indirectly to act swiftly in lodging his objection.

At this stage there is often a public inquiry into the proposals, but not necessarily so. If a local authority or river board objects there must be a public inquiry, but otherwise the holding of such an inquiry is at the discretion of the Secretary of State for the Environment. In practice there is almost always a public inquiry into any really major project, which gives everyone affected a chance to voice their objections either in person of through a lawyer or other representative. If no inquiry is held then all that the objector can do is send in a written objection giving reasons.

Once the overall plan has been approved the authority, public body, or other body empowered to make compulsory purchases, must send written notice to the owner of each piece of land which is to be bought. If the ownership of any particular plot is not known then a notice must be posted on the land. On receiving this formal notice the landowner may again object to the proposed compulsory purchase, but because by this time the plans have been approved anyway he has very little chance of succeeding in his objection, except perhaps in persuading them to make minor alterations. The kind of alteration which may be made following such objections are the reduction of the road width or re-alignment of a junction to reduce the encroachment on a garden and keep the road further from the house. The objection usually has to be made within three weeks of the date of the notice.

The Secretary of State will consider any objection made at this stage and may be able to agree on modifications of the plan which will satisfy the objector. If the objector is not satisfied then a hearing must be arranged before an inspector appointed by the Minister. Alternatively a public inquiry may be ordered, particularly if there are many objections and if there has been no public inquiry at an earlier stage. In that case the body or authority wishing to make the compulsory purchase must give to each objector the opportunity to state his reasons for the proposal about which he has objected. When the inquiry takes place only the people who have made formal objections, or their legal representative, have a right to give evidence or question the witnesses.

Once the objections have been dealt with and any hearing or inquiry has taken place the compulsory purchase order can be confirmed by the Minister. From this stage the price to be paid has to be decided, then the transfer of legal ownership can begin. A notice to treat is sent to each of the owners whose land is to be bought and they must then formulate their claims for the purchase and any compensation which may be payable.

3. Compensation

The procedure for assessing the purchase price and compensation is set in motion by the Notice to Treat sent to the owner. This notice must give particulars of the land to be bought, confirm that the purchasing body is prepared to negotiate the compensation to be paid, and ask for details of the owner's interest in the land and of his claim for compensation. As soon as he receives this notice the owner should act without delay. He has three weeks in which to notify the purchasing body of his intention to claim. If he does not do so within this period he may be unable to claim the costs of making the claim and negotiating the compensation. At this stage it is unlikely that he will be able to put any figure on the compensation he wants but he must tell them that he intends to claim.

Once he has done this the owner calculates the amount of his claim. Usually he will instruct a surveyor to value the property and negotiate on his behalf.

Provided that he has given notice of this claim in time the surveyor's fees, and also the legal fees for selling the property, are normally paid for him, this being a condition of the compulsory purchase order. In most cases there are many factors to be taken into account in assessing the price to be paid and the compensation may be allocated to several different grounds of claim.

The principal claim is, of course, for the value of the property to be purchased. This is now calculated according to the market value which the property will have if sold by a willing vendor to a willing purchaser. The fact that the owner does not wish to sell anyway and may be very reluctant to leave it is not to be taken into account to increase the price. But the fact that a property would have a particular attraction for certain people who would be prepared to pay an inflated price is relevant in deciding the price it would fetch. Unfortunately for the homeowner who is forced to sell, he is not allowed to take into account the fact that the Council, or whatever body is buying the land, has a scheme for developing the area including this property which makes the land more valuable as part of a development site.

The second item in calculating compensation is usually disturbance. Most compensation claims include a disturbance allowance because the owner has to move out of the property. Only in the case of the owner not being in possession because the property is let to a tenant, or is an empty building, or a vacant and unused piece of land, would this claim be unavailable. For the owner-occupier it includes the costs of removal to another house including the expenses of buying a replacement home such as legal charges, surveyor's fees, stamp duty and all the other usual expenses in addition to the actual cost of removing the furniture. However the payment for disturbance will only cover the purchase of a house of equivalent value; so an owner leaving a house worth £30,000 cannot get all the expenses of buying a replacement which costs £60,000.

If the homeowner also carried on a business from home the disturbance claim will include the expenses caused by his giving up the business or moving it to a new address. In addition to the cost of moving his stock and equipment he can claim for any loss in their value because of the move. Also he can claim the cost of printing new stationery, putting in new telephones, and other incidental costs of the move affecting his business. Most important however is his right to claim for loss of goodwill caused by his change of address, and the loss of profit caused by the disruption of moving.

As previously mentioned the owner's expenses of selling are a third ground of claim. These include the legal charges relating to the transfer of the legal title to the purchasing body. Also the fees of any agents or surveyors who act for the owner, advising him about the value, and even those fees for detailed negotiation with the purchasing body about various aspects of the claim are payable by them.

There are also several other grounds of claim which may or may not apply to any particular case. For example the value of any existing planning consent must be paid for if it increases the value of the property even though no action has yet been taken upon it. Then there may be a claim under the rather strange title of "injurious affection". This is a claim for the loss of value to the land still owned by the homeowner when part has been compulsorily purchased. A good example of this is when the front garden of a house has been compulsorily purchased for road widening. As part of his claim for compensation the owner can claim that the value of his property has been reduced, not just because the garden is smaller but because the traffic passes closer to the house bringing increased noise and dust.

Injurious affection can be claimed even when the homeowner has lost none of his land. There are many cases where some major construction work or alteration may affect a house which is nearby. The building of an airport or a motorway close to an existing house is almost certain to reduce the value of the property because of the noise it will bring. A sewage works constructed nearby could well knock thousands off the value of the house; while a new nuclear power station, in these days of concern about leaks of radioactivity, could well make nearby houses unsaleable. In all of these cases a claim for injurious affection is likely to result in compensation being awarded.

The owner can claim that the value has been reduced because the traffic passes closer to the house.

4. Planning blight

When a local authority or other public body has decided, or is even considering, a development plan which will involve a compulsory purchase of land, it becomes difficult for the owner to sell it. This is referred to as planning blight. At best, when the scheme is in an early stage of planning, the effect on a prospective purchaser who finds out about it will be to make him hesitant about buying the property in which he is interested. It may very well result in his making an offer much lower than he would otherwise have considered. When a proposed compulsory purchase will definitely affect the property in question, it becomes virtually unsaleable.

If property is affected in this way a homeowner may be able to force the body planning the compulsory purchase to buy his property now at its proper market value. To qualify, however, the owner must also be the occupier of the property and must have owned and occupied it for at least six months during the last eighteen months. An exception is allowed for the executors of an owner-occupier who has died and who wish to sell the property in the courses of winding up the estate.

A homeowner who wishes to sell and whose property is affected by planning blight can give notice to the body whose proposals affect the property. The notice demands that the body in question must buy the property at its full market price. Unless there are good grounds for refusing to buy the property the body must buy at a price agreed by them both or fixed by the Land Tribunal if they cannot agree. If the property is in fact outside the proposed compulsory area, or the owner does not have the right to force them to buy because he has not lived in the property for the required six months, then these are grounds for the purchasing body to refuse to buy. Another reason which allows them to refuse is that they do not plan to buy within the next fifteen years.

5. Highways and their adoption

To most people the word "highway" is usually thought of as referring only to a main road or motorway, but the legal meaning is quite different. In law the word "highway" includes motorways, main roads, country lanes, town streets, bridle paths, country footpaths, passageways in a town and even navigable rivers. The essential factor which all highways have in common is that all members of the public have a right to travel along or over them to get from one place to another, even if the only place they can get to is a house at the end of a cul-de-sac, or a field at the end of a country lane.

The vast majority of existing roads and streets in this country are public highways. A new major road built by the highway authority on land purchased for that purpose becomes a public highway as soon as it is opened for public use. When builders developing new housing estates obtain their planning consent it is generally made a condition of the consent that they must construct roads to the required standard which will then be adopted by the Council. An agreement is drawn up between the builders and the Council setting out how the road is to be constructed and what drainage and lighting is to be installed. The builders then agree with the owners of individual houses on the estate that they will construct the road and that the houseowners will not therefore be responsible for making up the roads. However not all houses are built next to a public highway and there are still a fair number of private roads which have never been adopted by the Council.

Until the Highway Authority, which may be either the County Council or the local District Council, officially adopts a road it will not be responsible for the repair and maintenance. This will remain the responsibility of the landowners whose lands border the road unless someone else has undertaken the burden. On a new housing estate the responsibility usually remains with the builder who undertakes to make up the roads until the Council takes them over. For older private roads there is in most cases, no agreement about road making or adoption. The owners of the properties adjoining a private road must therefore keep it in repair until the Council eventually decides to adopt it. When a Council does decide to adopt a previously unmade road the owners of the land on each side must pay the cost of making it up. The amount each has to pay depends upon the length of the frontage and in these days the cost to an ordinary house owner is likely to be between several hundred pounds and two or three thousand pounds depending upon the width of his garden where it joins the road.

The cost of making up the road at the front of a house may not be the worst of it. A corner house with an unmade road at the side often has a much longer boundary with that road and a correspondingly higher cost to be paid. When both the front road and the side road are not yet adopted the cost to the poor homeowner can be very high if the Council decides to make up both of them. The likelihood of having to pay roadmaking charges is one which anybody thinking of buying a house on an unmade road should bear in mind as it can sometimes seriously reduce the value of the house.

Even when all the proper roads are adopted the homeowner may not be entirely free of roadmaking charges. Occasionally a Council will decide to adopt a passageway leading to the back of terraced houses and once again the owners of the properties adjoining the passage have to pay for the cost of making it up.

6. Smoke control and other restrictions

In the distant past the homes in this country, like those throughout Europe, were heated by wood fires. At one time Britain was largely covered by forests and all that the homeowner had to do was to collect a store of logs during the summer which would keep the family warm through the winter. Naturally this could not last. Firstly the forests disappeared as more and more land came under the plough, and secondly the landowners began to fence in the woodlands which remained and to prevent the public from cutting the timbers. The winters became very cold indeed for most of the inhabitants of these islands, unless they were lucky enough to live in the vicinity of Newcastle-upon-Tyne.

The people of Newcastle had long ago discovered that the black stones which littered the beaches would burn surprisingly well; these stones they called sea-coal. Not only did it burn, but it produced more heat than wood and lasted longer in the fire. As the demand for this remarkable substance grew they began to dig in search of more, and so the coal mining industry began.

Before long the chimneys in the towns were belching forth black smoke. The people might be warmer in their houses, but outside the smoke combined with the natural fogs of winter to produce a black pall which settled over each town, cutting out the light, reducing visibility, and making any inhabitants who ventured out of doors cough and choke in the gritty atmosphere. Even so it was a long time before the real hazard to health was properly appreciated, and the Clean Air Act 1956 was passed.

Local authorities can now make an order declaring an area of smoke control. Anyone then emitting smoke from a chimney commits an offence, and the emission of black smoke is prohibited even before a smoke control order is made. However it is smoking chimneys which are banned, and the homeowner can still have a bonfire in his garden without running foul of the smoke control regulations. Of course a smoking bonfire can still be the source of a legal nuisance if the smoke drifts across neighbouring properties or public highways, particularly if it should cause an accident by reducing visibility on the roads.

When an order is made the Council has a duty to see that all houses in the smoke controlled zone have fireplaces, stoves, or other heating appliances which can burn smokeless fuel. The homeowner who has been happily burning coal in his open fireplaces can apply for a grant to convert the fireplaces, or replace them with others which can efficiently burn coke or other smokeless fuels. If he decides that he would rather have gas fires or electric fires or even instal a central heating system, he can do so, but in that case he must pay the extra cost if the price exceeds the grant to which he is entitled.

Under the Clean Air Act anyone emitting black smoke from a chimney may be prosecuted even when no smoke control order is in force. When a smoke control order has been made then the restrictions apply to any smoking chimneys whatever the colour of the smoke. The order also prohibits the burning in fireplaces or furnaces of any fuels except those which are declared to be "smokeless". They include gas, electricity, coke, anthracite and oil in authorised boilers or stoves.

Although smoke control orders are the most common restrictions imposed on the ordinary householder, there are a number of other controls which are not uncommon. There are of course general restrictions on any building work in an area which is declared to be "green belt" and even tighter controls within the National Parks. Many areas are also affected by orders controlling advertisements which prohibit erection of hoardings or the posting of advertisements on walls or other places.

Then there are tree preservation orders. A local authority may decide that it would be in the interest of the local community to preserve trees or woodlands in a particular area. It can achieve this by making a tree preservation order. The order includes a map on which the positions of the trees to be protected are marked. Once the order has been made a homeowner who has in his garden a protected tree cannot cut it down without the written consent of the Council. The restrictions go further because he cannot prune the tree by lopping the branches or "topping" it without the Council's consent. It can often take months to obtain the consent of the Council to any such proposals and the person applying will have to give good reasons for wishing to fell or lop the tree. However, exceptions are made for any trees which have died or become dangerous.

10

Mortgages, rates and other outgoings

1. The nature of a mortgage

A mortgage is an interest in property designed to protect a loan. All kinds of assets or goods may be mortgaged, but to most people the word "mortgage" means a loan on a house and that of course is the kind which interests us now. Alternative names are "legal charge" or simply "charge" which is the word officially used to describe a mortgage on land with a registered title. However it must be remembered that a mortgage is not the loan itself, but is the security given to the lender to make sure that his money will be safe.

The completion of a mortgage or legal charge creates a new legal interest in the property. The rights of the lender or "mortgagee" are not unlike the rights of a landlord of leasehold property. If the mortgage instalments or interest payments are not paid on the dates when they are due he has various rights and powers by which he can recover his money. The most important of these powers is the power of sale under which the mortgagee can obtain possession, ejecting the borrower and his family, then sell the house. Alternatively he may let the house to a tenant, collect the rents until the mortgage debt, including all interest and expenses, has been discharged, then hand the property back to the owner. Because of the problems attached to the letting of houses (see Chapter 11) this is an option rarely chosen nowadays by mortgagees.

In its earliest form a mortgage was a pledge for money loaned for a specific period, rather like a pledge of goods to a pawnbroker. The borrower had to make regular payments of interest but also had to repay the whole of the loan capital on the date written in the mortgage deed. If he failed to make the payment on the date specified then his rights to the property were forfeited and the mortgagee could keep the property for himself. This harsh rule was gradually modified and the courts developed new rules to control the rights of mortgagees. It became accepted that the transaction was basically a means of making sure that the mortgagee would not lose his money. Provided that the borrower repaid all that was due including all interest, even if payment were delayed until after the date in the deed, then he could keep his property. However the rights of the mortgagee were still protected if the borrower failed to pay what was due. In that case the mortgagee could apply to the court for the property to be transferred to him, or for it to be sold and the debt repaid.

With the development of building societies the idea of repaying the loan by instalments over a long period was introduced and this type of mortgage almost completely replaced the earlier loan for a fixed period. However even a mortgage payable by instalments often has a "legal date for redemption" which is the date on which it states that the whole of the loan will be repaid. This date is normally about three months after the date of the mortgage but of course no-one expects that the loan will actually be repaid on that date. The reason for including such a date is to make sure that the mortgagee will have the power of sale if the borrower then falls behind with any payment.

Building societies began as clubs in which the members each paid regular contributions. The funds collected were used to finance the building or purchase of houses which were then allocated to the members by a regular ballot. In time they changed the system of operating and began to lend the funds, collected as subscriptions from their members, to particular members who wanted to buy their own homes and who were prepared to pay a good rate of interest. This quickly became the main function of the building societies and is now regarded as the reason for their very existence.

Most mortgages these days provide for repayment by instalment over a fixed number of years, generally twenty years or twenty-five years. Each instalment paid is first applied to the payment of the interest due then anything left over is a reduction of the loan. In the early years the interest due takes up nearly all the instalments with only a small sum being paid off the capital, but as time passes the capital is reduced, the interest due becomes less each year and a greater part of each instalment goes towards paying off the capital.

An alternative method of repayment is by an endowment linked mortgage. The borrower borrows the money from the building society or insurance company for a fixed number of years and pays interest on the loan by monthly instalments. At the end of the period the whole loan must be repaid, but the money for this repayment is provided by an endowment life assurance policy. To make sure that the life policy money will come to them the mortgagees also take a mortgage on the policy so that the insurance company will pay the policy monies directly to the mortgagees when the policy matures at the end of the fixed mortgage period, or on the death of the borrower if he should die before that date. This type of mortgage usually results in the borrower paying a little more each month, in the interest payments and life policy premiums, than he would if he had a straightforward repayment mortgage. However it does have the following advantages:-

    1. Life cover is provided which will pay off the mortage if the borrower dies and this is an important factor for the head of a family (in fact a person

who simply wants life cover on the mortgage can obtain a special mortgage protection policy at a very cheap rate even with an ordinary repayment mortgage).

2. There is usually a bonus payable at the end of this period which will give the borrower a tax free cash sum after the mortgage has been repaid.

3. The borrower gets tax relief on the whole of the mortgage interest which does not reduce throughout the mortgage term. The endowment mortgage can therefore be advantageous particularly to the person with a larger mortgage, or a higher rate tax payer as is explained in section 2 of this Chapter.

In recent years the number of endowment mortgages has increased dramatically, partly because they give real benefits to certain borrowers and partly because borrowers are often pressurised into taking out life policies by agents or brokers who make large commissions on the new policies. One development which greatly assisted the insurance policy salesmen was the introduction of "low cost" or "build-up" life policies. The principle of the build-up policy is to make use of the large bonus usually added to a life policy each year. Instead of taking out a policy for the whole amount of the mortgage loan, the borrower takes out a smaller policy in the expectation of bonuses being added which will increase the value of the policy sufficiently to pay off the loan. For example, a borrower borrowing £10,000 from a building society might take out a policy for £5,000 plus bonuses payable at the end of 25 years. By the time the 25 years have passed the bonuses will probably have increased the value of the policy to about £12,500 so the borrower's mortgage is repaid and he gets a £2,500 cash payment. If the borrower dies before the 25 years are up then the policy guarantees to pay £10,000 anyway and this clears the mortgage. During the years of high inflation these "build-up" policies have shown good returns with the policy holders receiving large payments after the mortgage debts had been paid off. However the policies do not guarantee that the bonuses will necessarily be enough to pay off the mortgage debt, and the wise borrower will therefore have taken a policy providing estimated profits somewhat higher than seemed strictly necessary to meet the mortgage debt. Now that the annual rate of inflation has fallen to such a relatively low figure it remains to be seen what effect a low inflation rate, if maintained for several years, will have on the profits made by such a policy.

2. Tax relief on mortgage interest

Most people are aware that income tax relief is given to people with mortgages. From time to time certain politicians and others urge the Government to put an end to this "tax handout" to homeowners. It is to be hoped that whatever political party is in power from time to time, will resist this pressure because the boot is really on the other foot. The fact that homeowners with a mortgage are allowed tax relief is not so much because they are given a handout as because they are one of the categories of people still allowed to claim the tax relief which all borrowers once enjoyed.

Throughout most of the period of almost two hundred years since income tax was first introduced tax relief was allowed on all payments of loan interest. The principle was that the same money should not be taxed twice. If a man were under an obligation to pay loan interest then the person or company who received the payments had a legal right to be paid before the borrower used any of his income for himself. In effect that money was never his to spend. He was regarded as an intermediary collecting his income from his employers, or his customers if he were self-employed, and passing it on to the lender who, of course, paid tax upon it. The same principle still applies to a person who is under an obligation to pay an annuity or who makes payments under a Deed of Covenant.

In 1974 the Government of the day, in one of the periods when it wanted to slow down the economy, decided to tax the borrower on these interest payments. This increase had the advantage from the Government's point of view of slowing down the economy by making the borrowing of money more expensive, and at the same time producing a large amount of additional tax. On the other hand the poor borrower not only continues to pass a part of his income on to the lender but now has to pay tax upon it out of the rest of his income. Fortunately for the homeowner the Government realised then that the effect of taxing home loans would have been so severe that it would have upset the whole economy. It is not impossible that they also took into account the fact that a large percentage of the tax-paying public are also homeowners with mortgages, and that an enormous increase in their tax bills would have made that Government very unpopular. An exception was therefore made for mortgage interest, within certain limits, along with interest on certain business loans.

The restrictions which now apply to a mortgage loan on a private house, if it is to qualify for tax relief on the interest, are as follows:-

1. The loan must have been made for the purchase or improvement of the home.
2. It must be the borrower's only, or principal home.
3. The tax relief will only apply on a loan up to a certain amount. This changes from time to time but the present limit for relief is £30,000.

Most mortgage loans are of course obtained for the sole purpose of buying a house. These get full tax relief up to £30,000. Sometimes a homeowner will wish to improve his house by building an extension, or installing central heating. A loan for such improvements again falls within the rules and will receive tax relief on the interest. However the person who borrows just enough money to buy the house then wishes to borrow extra money so that he can buy furniture or a new car, or even to pay a decorator for painting the house, will not get tax relief on the second loan. It is worth thinking about what extra money may later be needed when deciding upon how much mortgage money should be borrowed. A larger mortgage loan at that stage will qualify for tax relief and the borrower can then keep some of his own money in a bank or building society investment account until he needs it to buy his car or his carpets.

Tax relief is not given for a loan on a second home. A homeowner who has two houses can obtain tax relief on the mortgage interest paid for the principal home only. For this purpose a husband and wife living together are treated as one person and can claim tax relief on only one mortgage even though the husband owns one house and the wife the other, each paying their own mortgage interest. Only in the event of a genuine separation can they claim relief on both mortgages on the basis that they are maintaining two separate and distinct households. However a homeowner who borrows money to buy a house for occupation by a dependent relative (e.g. his widowed mother) can claim tax relief on the interest paid on that loan as well as on the mortgage loan on his own house.

When a homeowner is changing houses it may be necessary for him to have two houses for a time. This provides an exception to the general rule. A borrower who completes the purchase of a new house, before completing the sale of the old one, can claim tax relief on the interest paid under both the old mortgage and the new mortgage or bridging loan. The limit of £30,000 applies in that case to the loan on each house for a period of up to one year. During that period the owner may claim tax relief on the two loans, which together could be considerably more than the normal limit of £30,000. However the limit in this case is £30,000 on each house, and if one of the loans should be less than £30,000 the borrower cannot claim the surplus relief on the other loan, even though that might be greater than £30,000.

There is another exception in the case of second property which is let on a commercial basis. Interest paid on a loan obtained for the purposes of buying an investment property can be deducted from the rent received so that only the balance of the rent is taxed. This relief also extends to the homeowner who has a country cottage or other holiday home (including a large permanent caravan or houseboat) which he uses himself for holidays but also lets to other people. He can offset the mortgage interest he pays upon it against the rent he receives, but it is a condition of this relief that the holiday home must be let, or offered for letting, for at least half the year.

At one time mortgage interest was paid gross with the relief being given to the borrower in his tax code, if he paid PAYE tax, or on his annual tax return for a self-employed borrower. For most homeowners with mortgages the system was changed with the introduction of MIRAS (Mortgage Interest Relief At Source). Previously the homeowner received tax relief by having a reduction in the tax he paid, while the building society paid the tax on the interest it received. In the case of a homeowner whose mortgage is subject to MIRAS the emphasis has shifted. He now pays tax in full, but pays a reduced amount to the building society. This change in procedure has the benefit of allowing the person on a low income to benefit from the reduced interest, replacing the earlier and more cumbersome system by which he had to claim a reduction in his interest payments.

The MIRAS scheme does not apply to all mortgages because the borrowers with bigger mortgages do not, of course, get tax relief on all the interest they pay. In general they must still pay their interest gross, then claim a reduction in their tax payments for the interest on the first £30,000. However some, but not all, building societies will now split the loan, allowing the borrower to have the benefit of the MIRAS relief on the first £30,000 of the loan, while still paying gross interest on the balance.

3. Powers of a mortgagee

The powers of a mortgagee are now laid down in Acts of Parliament. The principal rights are:-

   (a) The right to sell the property.
   (b) The right to appoint a receiver.
   (c) The right to foreclose.
   (d) The right to insure the property.
   (e) The right to hold the Title Deeds.

In addition the mortgage deed usually gives the mortgagee additional rights such as a right to sue the borrower for payment of monies due under his covenants, and a right to carry out repairs to the property at the expense of the borrower.

As previously mentioned the power of sale given to the mortgagee is his most important right. If the borrower falls two months behind with the mortgage payments or breaks his covenants, or fails to repay the mortgage loan after being given proper notice requiring him to repay it, then the mortgagee may sell the property. In practice a mortgagee of a private house occupied by the borrower and his family would normally apply to the court first to obtain possession so that the property can be sold with vacant possession, but the mortgagee has the right to sell without any application to the court. Of course the borrower can prevent the sale by paying to the mortgagee all principal and interest due under the mortgage but he must also repay to the mortgagee all costs and expenses incurred by the mortgagee in enforcing the debt.

Once a property has been sold by the mortgagee he becomes a trustee so far as the purchase money is concerned. The money is first applied in paying off the mortgages on the property. If there are two or more mortgages they are paid off in the order in which they were created. The mortgagee also retains the costs and expenses of the sale. After these payments have been made any surplus belongs to the borrower and is paid over to him.

The right of foreclosure is rarely used these days. It is the right for the mortgagee to keep the property himself rather than to sell it. There are, however, several disadvantages for him. Firstly it can only be exercised by obtaining an order of the court. When the court makes the order it must give the borrower time to raise the money elsewhere and pay off the debt. The normal time allowed for this is six months, so the mortgagee has a longer time to wait before he can get back his money. Secondly there are circumstances in which the borrower can still get his property back by paying off the mortgage debt even after the ownership has been transferred to the mortgagee. This makes it difficult for the mortgagee to sell the property later because a purchaser might find that he has to give it up again. Thirdly the mortgagee cannot sue the borrower for any surplus if the price he receives when he sells the property is less than the debt due to him. And lastly the court may order that the property should be sold anyway if it decides it is fairer to the borrower to do this.

The power of appointing a receiver is more appropriate to the mortgage of a commercial property producing substantial rents. In that case the receiver collects the rents from the tenants until the mortgage is repaid. This right is rarely used by a mortgagee of a private house.

4. General rates and water rates

General rates are a form of local taxation. They are assessed on the notional letting value of buildings, but not land. The rateable value on a new building is decided by a local valuation officer, and from time to time the whole of property in the country or in a particular part of the country is reassessed and brought up to date. Because this is such an immense undertaking it happens only once in about thirty years.

In addition to assessing the rateable value of a new building the local valuation offier is instructed to visit any building which has been extended or altered and reassess its value. Such a reassessment is made when a building is divided into parts, as for example upon the conversion of a house into flats, when each flat is then assessed as a separate unit. Similarly an assessment is made when the flats are reconverted to become a single house, or two small cottages are converted into one large one.

Any homeowner who disagrees with the assessment of his house is entitled to appeal against it. The local authority will consider the reasons he gives for his objection and may offer to make a reduction in the rateable value if it considers them justified. If he accepts the reduction offered, then the reduced figure will become the new rateable value registered against the property. If the local authority will not reduce the rateable value, or will not agree to reduce it by as much as the homeowner wants, he can apply for it to be decided by the Land Tribunal.

There are no specific grounds laid down upon which the rateable value of a property should be reduced but all matters which might affect the value can be taken into account. The most common grounds upon which people appeal against the valuation are firstly a comparison between the house and others of similar kind or size in the vicinity which are assessed at a lower figure; and secondly external factors which affect the value of this particular property. An appeal is often made when changes are made in the use of neighbouring land which result in a loss of value, or make it less pleasant to live in the house. The construction of a motorway close to a house, the building of an industrial complex across the road, or the construction of a new runway at an airport two miles away which results in the house being directly under the flightpath are all good grounds for a rating appeal.

Once the rateable values have been assessed they form the basis for calculating the general rates payable by the homeowner. The local authority knowing the total value of the properties in its area can adjust the amount of its income each year by fixing a rate of so many pence in the pound. For example a house may have a rateable value of £400; if the local authority fixes a rate of 120 pence in the pound the occupier pays £1.20 for each pound of the rateable value, i.e. £480 for the year.

There are however a number of variable factors in the collection of the rates. If a house is occupied by an old age pensioner with a low income or a family on supplementary benefit a rate rebate is given and a reduced sum is payable. Also if the house is unoccupied and unfurnished for a time then no general rates are payable for at least part of that period. It used to be the rule that no rates were paid on an empty house no matter how long it remained vacant but a few years ago local authorities were given the right to charge rates on a vacant house after a certain time. Most local authorities have now adopted this rule and usually rates become payable after the property has been empty for more than three months.

General rates are payable by the occupier of a house rather than the owner. When a house is let to a tenant it is the tenant who is responsible for payment and the local authority will sue him if the rates are unpaid. However there are many tenancies, particularly of houses or flats, where the landlord accepts responsibility for the rates and in that case the tenant can reclaim the money from the landlord if he is forced to pay the rates to the council. Also it should be remembered that the rates are charged on the *occupier*, not on the property. When a house is sold and the new owner moves in he will be responsible for the rates only from the date when he takes possession and cannot be made responsible for the period when it was occupied by the former owner, unless he has agreed with the former owner to accept that responsibility and the council have been notified of the arrangement. This is the opposite of the situation which exists for ground rent where the leasehold owner for the time being is always responsible for all arrears of ground rent even when he has only just bought the property.

As a form of taxation to raise the income required by local authorities the rating system is inefficient, unjust, unpopular and in urgent need of replacement. The system is difficult to administer with constant reassessments being required by specialist property valuers, but on a basis which is highly artificial anyway and subject to challenge by the occupiers on a variety of grounds. There are too many variables with rates rebates, empty property rates, industrial rates and frequent adjustments and apportionments being required. The injustice is all too obvious when a widow living alone in the house which has been her family home for many years must pay the same amount as the family of six people in the identical house next door who are all in full time employment and all enjoying in full the services provided by the local authority and paid for out of the rates. Governments and political parties have for decades been promising reform and replacement of the rating system but keep postponing it because of the problems which any alternative kind of local taxation would create. However, the present Government has recently made a commitment to reform the system, and it will be interesting to see what comes of it. Certainly one would think it possible to devise a new system which would be superior to the old one.

Water rates are even less justifiable than general rates. The only reason for making a charge for water based on the rateable value appears to be that because rateable values exist they provide a convenient way of levying a charge for the supply of water without the trouble and expense of providing all properties with water meters. If everyone paid for the water they actually used they would be far less likely to waste it and there would be more incentive to replace defective washers or ball valves. It is high time that all properties were fitted with water meters and the supply of water paid for on the basis of the quantity used.

For the time being however, the water rating system is administered in much the same way as general rates. The charge is upon the occupier, but no water rates are payable on an empty house no matter how long it remains empty.

When a house is sold it is the usual practice these days for both water rates and general rates to be apportioned by the Water Board and the local authority and for apportioned demand notes to be issued to the outgoing owner and the incoming owner each calculated on the number of days of occupation.

It is not widely appreciated that the owner of a house may apply to the Water Board for his supply of water to be metered. A charge will not normally be made by the Board for supplying a meter but the homeowner will have to pay a plumber to instal it. For anyone with a high rateable value, especially if the house has only two or three people in residence, this is well worth considering as it will probably result in a substantial saving.

5. Electricity, gas and telephones

The supply of electricity and gas, and also the connection and use of a telephone, are not related to the ownership or occupation of a house. They are simply commercial transactions and the person liable for payment is the one who enters an agreement with the electricity board, gas board, and telephone company. It is important to remember this especially when selling a house or leaving a rented property.

When a person buys a house or rents one he should contact the local electricity board, and the gas board and telephone company if appropriate, signing their forms for a supply. If he fails to do this early enough he may find that the supply has been cut off when the previous owner left, and if that happens he will be charged an extra fee for reconnecting them. Remember that it is not the owner or the tenant or the head of the household who must pay for the electricity, gas etc., but the person who signs the forms. The accounts will be issued in his name and he will be sued if they are not paid. This will continue until the appropriate board is notified otherwise. A homeowner who omits to tell them that he is selling his house and to request them to make a final reading of the meter will remain legally responsible for payment for electricity and gas used, and telephone calls made, even after he has left.

6. Insurance

For the majority of homeowners with mortgages on their houses the insurance is arranged and maintained by their building society or other mortgagee. In that case the premium payments will usually be demanded once a year by the building society but in some cases they are included in the monthly mortgage payments. In most cases where the building society covers the property the homeowners will have arranged their own private insurance cover on their household contents, but where there is no mortgage it is usually more convenient to have a household insurance policy which covers both the house and contents. Whatever the insurance arrangements may be the homeowner should never forget how important the insurance of both house and contents is and that the amount covered should be regularly reviewed.

Many people who buy a house are surprised at the insurance figure put upon it by the building society. Frequently it is much higher than the price actually paid for the house. Many older houses offer more accommodation in both the number and size of rooms than a modern house just completed by a builder which is offered for sale at the same price. Although the homeowner may feel that in the event of his house being completely destroyed by fire or some other disaster he could buy another similar house at the same price, the insurance companies do not look at it in this way. Their obligation is to rebuild or repair the original house exactly as it was, and the cost will include the demolition of the ruins of the original house, the clearance of the site and the employment of an architect to prepare plans for rebuilding, as well as the actual cost of reconstruction. This may have serious consequences in the case of a claim for the repair or partial rebuilding of the existing house, and it must be remembered that it is comparatively rare for a house to be completely destroyed.

If the property is under-insured the insurance company can claim that the owner has opted to accept part of the risk himself.

Unless the sum covered by the insurance policy is sufficient to cover the cost of completely rebuilding the original house and buildings, the insurance company can claim that the property is under-insured and that the owner has opted to accept part of the risk himself. Thus in the case of a house being covered for £40,000, which may have been the price paid for it, when the cost of rebuilding would be £60,000, the insurance company could claim that it has accepted responsibility for only two thirds of the risk. In that case if a fire were to break out at that house causing damage which cost £12,000 to repair, the insurance company would pay only £8,000 and the owner would have to find the remaining £4,000 himself. This is a risk which no homeowner is likely to want to take once he understands it. He should therefore check from time to time on the amount he has covered and make sure that it keeps pace with the inflation in the cost of house building. A purchaser who buys a house without the aid of a mortgage should carefully consider the amount of cover and if he has any doubts about it he may ask the insurance company to inspect it and tell him what they consider to be its replacement value.

When a person buys another house he should arrange insurance cover before he exchanges contracts for the purchase. The purchaser who is under contract to buy must complete his purchase and pay the agreed price on the date agreed even though the house has been destroyed or damaged in the meantime. For this reason a building society making a mortgage offer usually arranges immediate insurance cover on the house, but a purchaser who is not borrowing money on mortgage may well overlook this. If he has not already completed an insurance proposal form and obtained a new policy before the contracts are exchanged he should arrange temporary immediate cover on exchanging contracts. On no account should he ask the insurance company to transfer the cover from his old house to his new one, which would leave his old one without cover. It is far better to obtain a completely new policy on the new house, then claim a refund of the unexpired part of the premium paid on the old house when the sale of that property is completed.

Lettings and lodgers

1. Letting a house

Tenancies of private houses, and in particular the right of an owner to regain possession, have in general been subject to restrictions since 1920. The history of rent control and the security of tenure given to residential tenants since then is extremely complex. There have been frequent changes in the detail of the restrictions placed on the landlord, sometimes giving more powers to a landlord to increase the rent or remove an unsatisfactory tenant, but at other times increasing the protection given to a tenant. However, the present situation is that the majority of residential tenants of houses or flats, both furnished and unfurnished, enjoy a security of tenure which was unknown in earlier times. The consequence for the landlord is usually a serious drop in the value of his property as he can no longer obtain vacant possession and the rent he receives has in most cases fallen far behind the general level of inflation.

Fortunately for the owner-occupier of a private house or flat there are now a number of special provisions which put him in a better position than the owner of a property acquired for commercial letting. The owner-occupier may let his house if he goes abroad or to another part of the country on business, and recover possession when he returns home. Alternatively he may let rooms or flats within the house without saddling himself with a tenant who can stay there forever. There is also the possibility of letting the house or flat for short periods to holiday makers without creating a protected tenancy.

As this book is concerned with the homeowner, and particularly the owner-occupier, this chapter deals principally with lettings by an owner-occupier. The position of lodgers is also considered, as is the letting of a second home used for holidays or bought as a retirement home. Properties bought as an investment do not come within these categories, and the special provisions do not apply to them.

Whether a house or other property is owner-occupied, a holiday home, or otherwise, the owner should be extremely wary of arranging any sort of letting, tenancy, or licence to occupy, no matter for how short a period. The fact that the proposed tenant or licensee is well known to the owner, perhaps even a close friend, and wants the use of the property, or part of the property, for only a very short period, should not be allowed to cloud the judgement. The effect of an unwise letting can be so serious for the owner that he should always take legal advice before entering into any such agreement, and should insist on having the tenancy agreement or other contract professionally drawn up.

2. Letting one's own house

Special provisions were introduced in 1965 to allow an owner-occupier to let his own home for a limited period. Until then anyone wishing to let his own house was treated in exactly the same way as a landlord who owned and let houses for profit, so that the tenant would become protected by the various Rent Acts and the owner would be unable to regain possession. This caused particular hardship to the person who was sent abroad on business for two or three years and who wished to come back to his own house at the end of that time. He did not dare to let the house while he was away for fear that for a very long period he might lose the right to occupy it. Therefore he had to choose between selling it, or leaving it standing empty and unused until he returned. The new rules applying to an owner-occupier gave him an absolute right to get the house back when he needed it. He can now safely let the house so that it will remain occupied during his absence, and the rent will pay his mortgage instalments, rates and other outgoings.

To obtain the benefit of the special provisions for owner-occupiers the person letting his house must himself have been in residence at the house. Before he lets it he must give written notice to the tenant that he is the owner-occupier and that he is entitled to regain possession. If the tenant gives up the tenancy before the owner returns the house can be let to another tenant, but again written notice must be given to the new tenant that the landlord is the owner-occupier. The benefit of these special rights of the landlord will be lost unless each letting since the owner was himself in residence has been on this special basis and the appropriate written notice given to each tenant in turn. It is therefore most important that this should never be overlooked when a new letting is arranged. In fact the notice may be contained in a letter to the tenant beforehand or in the written tenancy agreement itself. Of course in the latter case it is essential that the tenancy agreement is signed by the tenant before he is allowed into possession. In practice the safest procedure is *always* to include the notice in the tenancy agreement and *never* to let the tenant into possession until the agreement has been signed.

When the owner returns from his spell abroad, or from wherever he has been, he can give the tenant notice to quit. The notice must of course be in accordance with the terms of the letting, and for this reason it is often wise to let the house on a periodic tenancy (e.g. on a monthly basis so that it can be brought to an end by one month's notice) rather than for a fixed number of years, in case the owner wishes to return unexpectedly early. The tenant must then give up his tenancy and if he does not do so the owner can obtain an order for possession from the court. Provided that the correct procedure has been followed the court has no discretion about this and must order the tenant to vacate the property. In fact the court can exercise its discretion to order that the house be returned to the owner even if the owner has failed to give the proper notices before letting the house but obviously it is better to avoid this uncertainty.

The grounds upon which the owner can regain possession are any of the following:-

1. That he wants it for his own occupation
2. That some member of his family who was living with the owner at the house when he last occupied it now wishes to live in it.
3. That the owner has died and the house is now required as a residence for some member of his family who was living with him when he last occupied it.
4. That the owner has died and the person now entitled to ownership either wants to live in it or wishes to sell it with vacant possession.
5. That the mortgagee who had a mortgage before the property was let to the tenant wishes to sell it under the mortgagee's power of sale.
6. That the house is no longer suitable for the owner because of his present place of work and he needs to sell it so that he can use the proceeds of sale to buy another house more suitable to his needs.

There are no special conditions as to the reason why the owner occupier decides to let his house. It may be because his employers require him to live at his place of work, or his employment takes him abroad, or to another part of this country, or because he decides to go on a world cruise. The simple fact that he has been in occupation himself and now wishes to let the house is sufficient to give him the right to regain possession.

Similar special provisions apply to a member of the armed forces letting his own house, and to the letting of an owner-occupied house to an agricultural tenant.

3. The holiday home

The homeowner may have a second house for holiday use. He may even live permanently at the seaside or in some other part of the country where there is a demand for holiday letting. In either case he may wish to let the house, or part of it, to holiday makers when he and his family are not using it. Such holiday lettings do not give the tenant any protection under the Rent Acts or a right to

The courts are wary of a tenancy being created under the guise of a holiday letting which is a sham.

occupy the property for any period beyond the agreed time of the holiday. The holiday tenant does, of course, have his right under the contract to use the property during the agreed holiday period, but he must move out immediately at the end of that time.

The courts are wary of a tenancy being created under the guise of a holiday letting which is a sham. If the court believes that the letting is not in fact for a holiday, even though the letting agreement states that it is for holiday purposes, then it may award the tenant a protected tenancy. Most holiday lettings are so obviously for holiday purposes, as for example when a cottage in Cornwall is let for two weeks in August to a tenant from London, that no suggestion of a sham could possibly arise. However a house let in Manchester for a period of six months to a tenant whose previous home was in neighbouring Salford, would raise grave doubts no matter how carefully the so-called holiday letting agreement was worded.

Apart from the question of security of tenure the amount of rent payable can be of the greatest importance in a holiday letting. The protected tenant can apply for registration of his tenancy, and if the rent he is paying is excessive he can have it reduced. No such restrictions apply to holiday lettings. The owner can ask for as much rent as anyone is prepared to pay and once the agreement has been signed the tenant is legally bound to pay it.

There is another benefit to the owner of a holiday home who wants to let it out of season. Provided that the property has been let for holiday purposes at some time during the year it can be let to a tenant off-season for a fixed period of not more than eight months without the full restrictions of the Rent Acts affecting it. Again the owner *must* give written notice to the tenant, before the tenancy commences, that he has the right to regain possession, as in the case of an owner-occupier letting his own house. Once more it is important that the tenant should not be allowed into possession before the tenancy agreement is signed. If the correct procedures are followed the tenant will not be allowed to remain in occupation when the letting comes to an end.

To obtain the benefit of this exception the owner must be able to prove that he had let the property on holiday lettings during the previous twelve months. The fact that the owner and/or his family used it themselves as a holiday home during that period is not sufficient. However the use of the property by the owner himself for holidays does not prevent him benefitting from this exception so long as he also lets it to others on holiday lettings during the year.

For the effect of Income Tax, Capital Gains Tax and VAT on holiday homes and holiday lettings, see Chapter 14.

4. The retirement home

The homeowner letting his own home has been taken care of, but what about the person working abroad who wants to buy a house in this country for his or her retirement? Also the employee who presently must live at his place of work, or simply someone who sees the ideal retirement home in the country and wants to buy it now, may be concerned about the effect of letting their dream home to tenants. They need not be because there are similar provisions to protect their lettings.

The owner who has bought his retirement home and now wants to let it on a temporary basis to a tenant, may also give the tenant notice of his right to regain possession. In this case the right only applies when the owner actually retires from his regular employment (unless of course he dies first or the mortgagees wish to sell the property, in which case the right to regain possession applies as in the case of a letting by an owner-occupier). As before, the notice must be given to the tenant in writing before the tenancy commences, or may be included in the letting agreement. Again it is advisable to *always* include the notice in the letting agreement and to make sure that a new tenant *never* takes possession before the agreement is signed and exchanged.

There is some doubt about the exact meaning of the words "regular employment" and it has been suggested that this may not include the self-employed. Such a restricted interpretation would seem to be most unreasonable, and probably incorrect, but any self-employed person thinking of letting his intended retirement home should first consult a solicitor and ask him to make sure that there has been no recent decision made by the courts on this particular point. Another case which may cause problems and in which legal advice should certainly be sought is where the retirement home is jointly owned by a husband and wife, either or both of whom may be in regular employment at the time of the letting. It is in any case always advisable for anyone thinking of letting a house whatever the circumstances may be, to obtain legal advice about the particular proposed letting, and to have the tenancy agreement professionally drawn up.

5. Letting part of the house

Another case in which special provisions apply for the benefit of the homeowner is on the letting of part of his house. He may own a house which is now too big for him because his family has grown up and left home. Alternatively he may have bought a large house, to convert it into flats which he can then let to produce an income. In each case the special provisions will apply to him provided that he is himself resident in part of the building. But the provisions do not apply to a custom built block of flats.

The reason for this exception to the general rules, giving security to tenants, is that the personality and behaviour of a tenant living in the same building can be very important to the owner. A bad tenant might make his life a misery. He is therefore allowed to terminate the tenancy by a notice to quit in accordance with the terms of the tenancy. If the tenant does not leave after being given notice to quit the owner can obtain an order for possession from the court. However, the court does have a certain amount of discretion in this case. It may order that the date for possession be suspended for three months, even though the correct date is given in the notice to quit in accordance with the tenancy agreement.

The tenant also has the right to refer the question of rent to the Rent Tribunal, the body which controls lettings in general. The Rent Tribunal will decide what is a fair rent for the premises let and will register that rent. Once a rent has been registered it becomes the maximum figure which the owner can charge for the premises which are let, even if he terminates the tenancy and re-lets to a new tenant. Only by a new application to the Rent Tribunal can he increase the rent.

The homeowner may avoid some of the effects of the Rent Acts by sharing some "essential living rooms" with the tenant. Protection for the tenant under the Rent Act only applies when the tenant has "exclusive possession" of his flat or apartment. Where the tenancy includes a right to use a kitchen or other living room jointly with the landlord it ceases to be a letting of a wholly separate dwelling. The disadvantage, of course, is that the homeowner must share an even closer relationship with the tenant, and if he finds it difficult to get on with him life can become very difficult until he gets an order for possession from the court. Surprisingly a bathroom or a lavatory are not for this purpose regarded as "essential living rooms" and the sharing of them will not prevent the tenant from having the protection of the Rent Acts.

The rules applying to the letting of a flat by a landlord in residence apply equally to a landlord living in the building who is just one of two or more joint owners, but special care must be taken in the wording of a tenancy agreement in such a case. They also apply to a landlord who is away for a large part of the time because he is a seaman, or an oil rig worker, or otherwise frequently away on business. It is even possible for a person with two houses who spends his time divided between them to claim that he is a landlord in residence so long as he is genuinely in residence at this particular property for a substantial part of the year.

In all these cases the terms of the letting and the wording of the tenancy agreement may be absolutely crucial. Anyone considering entering into such a letting would be foolish to do so without first seeking legal advice and having the letting agreement professionally drawn.

6. Lodgers

There is a marked difference between the standing of a tenant and a lodger. A tenant has a right of possession and occupation whether he has a long lease or one of the restricted tenancies mentioned in this chapter. On the other hand a person who is a lodger, paying guest, or hotel guest has simply a licence to stay at the property. The tenant may have security which will enable him to stay at the property indefinitely, and at the worst is entitled to receive notice of a particular length, and his right to remain in the property will be protected by the courts. The lodger may be entitled to compensation if the owner orders him out in breach of an agreement they have made, but the careful owner agreeing to take in a lodger will make sure that he retains the right to end the agreement at any time.

There are no restrictions imposed by the law on the amount payable by a lodger, unlike the situation of a tenant when in most cases the rent may be fixed by outsiders, and the difference in the nature of the arrangement produces other effects. A tenant can keep the owner of the property out of his flat or room and can change the lock to make sure that no-one else can get in. On the other hand the owner of the property is allowed access to the room of a lodger and cannot be prevented from entering it at any reasonable time. Also the owner can exercise more control over the lodger and his use of the property, as in restricting visitors to the lodger's room. But the benefits are not all one way. For example the owner has a greater responsibility to a lodger so far as security of his possessions is concerned, and if he does not take adequate precautions may be liable for damages if things are stolen from a lodger's room.

It is not always easy to decide whether someone is a tenant or a lodger. Most cases are of course quite clear but there is a grey area in the middle. There are a number of pointers which indicate one way or the other such as:-

(a) Does the flat or room have its own cooking facilities and/or bathroom?
(b) Are meals provided?
(c) Is a cleaning service provided for the room or flat?
(d) Is the arrangement on a daily basis, weekly, monthly, or something else?
(e) Is the period of notice specified?
(f) Is electricity and/or heating provided free?
(g) Does the landlord or owner have a key?
(h) Are visitors allowed or not?
(i) Is the flat furnished?

Usually the answers to these questions will be absolutely conclusive in deciding whether a person is a tenant or a lodger. However where there is a conflict between them and there is real doubt then the acid test is the question of control. A tenant has complete control over his own premises and can keep out everyone including the landlord during the period of his tenancy, although he may be required under his covenants to allow the landlord to enter from time to time in order to see the state of repair or for other specific reasons. On the other hand a lodger cannot prevent the owner from entering the premises and cannot refuse to let the owner keep a key which will give him access.

The fact that the tenant shares a sitting room, bathroom, or kitchen with the landlord or other tenants is not in itself greatly significant. Even though he does share or use these common rooms, a person can still have exclusive occupation and possession of his own room and so becomes a tenant of that room.

Trespassers, visitors and others

1. Trespass

Forgive us our trespasses! Why, one might ask, was Our Lord so concerned about trespass that he referred to it in the Prayer he taught His followers, which became the most significant prayer in the whole Christian religion? Was the social structure of His time threatened by people wandering in larger numbers over the land of their neighbours? The answer of course is that the word "trespass" had a much wider meaning at the time when the authorised translation of the Bible was prepared at the order of King James I. In those days its meaning was simply a wrong done to another person, and virtually all civil actions in the law courts of those days were based upon trespass. There was trespass to the person, now replaced by assault and battery, and trespass to goods, as well as trespass to land. Even the words "trespass to land" included all manner of wrongs against the land of another person which have since been largely replaced by other rights of action. So we are left with the meaning of the word which is familiar to everyone now, unlawful entry upon, or occupation of, the land of another, as the only trespass which is still of major importance.

"Trespassers will be prosecuted" is the other common usage of the word, familiar to the public because it appears on notice boards all over the country. This is equally misleading. The vast majority of trespassers cannot be prosecuted in the criminal courts. There are exceptions, where trespass on certain Crown lands or Government properties has been made a criminal act, but for the ordinary citizen whose land is invaded the only redress is a private action for ejection or for damages. This was brought home to most people recently when a "hippy convoy" descended upon the fields of a farmer and set up camp there. The police were helpless to do anything about it until the landowner had obtained an order from the court to expel them. Following this case there has been talk of making trespass to land, or at least certain types of trespass, a criminal act. So who knows, we may yet see the day when the trespasser on private land can be prosecuted!

2. Trespassers before the courts

One of the reasons why trespass to land is still of major importance is because it gives the landowner an immediate, but private, legal right of action against the trespasser. It is no use for the trespasser to claim that he did not know he was trespassing, or that he had lost his way, or even that he genuinely thought the land was his own. The very fact that he has entered the land of another person without permission is enough to make him a trespasser. There used to be some doubt about whether a person who went upon another's land involuntarily, as by falling over a wall or being thrown over the hedge by his horse, was a trespasser. It is now fairly certain that he is not unless he arrived on the land as a result of his own negligence, for example by crashing through the hedge in his car because he took a bend too fast.

Given the fact that a person is trespassing, or has trespassed, on his property the homeowner may take action against him in the courts. If trespassers are still on the land, as in the case of the "hippy convoy", then he can apply for an injunction to have them removed. Where a trespasser frequently enters on the land the owner can ask the court to grant an injunction to prohibit that trespasser from entering the land again. If the trespasser disobeys such an injunction then he could be sent to prison or fined.

Whether the court grants an injunction or not the landowner may ask, or the court may decide, that the trespasser should pay compensation to the landowner by way of damages. Damages can be awarded regardless of whether the trespass is continuing or was simply a single act of entry on the land lasting only a few minutes. Once a trespass has been established, then the owner has proved that a wrong has been done to him, and the court may give him damages. A warning note must be sounded here, however, before any homeowner who has seen his neighbour walk across his land rushes to the court expecting to receive compensation. The courts will not encourage trivial claims and, even though he succeeds in a claim for damages, the owner who is too anxious to make a claim for a trivial offence might find that the cost to him is very high while the trespasser gets away virtually scot free.

Damages awarded by a court can fall into any one of several categories. To begin with there is the straightforward award of damages as compensation for the loss which has been suffered. In the case of trespass to land this might be assessed as either the reduction in the value of the land or buildings as a result of the injury caused, or as the cost of repairing the damage. The court will decide which is appropriate in a particular case. However the court can take into account the behaviour of all the parties concerned and may increase the damages if the trespasser has behaved in a particularly offensive way. On the other hand it may grant only nominal or even "contemptuous" damages. When a trespasser has caused real damage to the land or buildings, or having entered the land refuses to leave, then the landowner has enough reason for taking court proceedings and is likely to get satisfaction. The court will usually make an order for damages to be paid to him for compensation and order the trespasser to leave the property, or not to enter it again, if this should be necessary. In such a case the court is also likely to order that all the legal costs of the land owner should be paid by the trespasser. However, it is possible that even in a case when damages are awarded the court may decide that the landowner has himself created or been largely responsible for the situation and may therefore refuse to grant him an order for his costs. Of course there may always be a problem for the successful owner who is given damages and costs in getting paid. If the trespasser is a vagrant or some other person with no capital assets and little income, actually making him pay the damages and costs may in the end prove impossible.

In cases when the trespasser has behaved in a particularly offensive or outrageous way the court may order "aggravated damages" or occasionally "exemplary damages", against him. Aggravated damages are given as compensation to the owner for injury to his proper feelings of pride and dignity. For example they could be awarded against a trespasser who behaved in an insolent and high handed manner, or who threatened physical violence to the owner or his family, even though no actual damage had been caused to the land or buildings. Exemplary damages may occasionally, and in certain cases, be awarded as a punishment against a trespasser, although punishment is normally handed out by the criminal law rather than in a private action for damages.

At the opposite extreme there are cases where an odd act of trespass takes place where no injury is caused to the land, including the crops, trees, or plants growing on it, or the building, walls, fences or gates. Even though a legal wrong has been suffered by the owner he should think very carefully about it before deciding to take the matter to court. At most he is likely to receive nominal damages perhaps £1 or £5 and he may have to pay his own legal charges and expenses of the proceedings. If the court believes that his behaviour at the time was reprehensible, or that he himself created the situation which led to the trespass, or that in the cirumstances no claim should ever have been made by him, then it may award contemptuous damages. While admitting that he is legally entitled to claim against the trespasser it can award only one penny as damages and may even order that he should pay all the costs of the trespasser, as well as his own costs. In that case the cost to the owner of enforcing his legal rights could be very high indeed.

3. Self help

The landowner whose property is entered by a trespasser may expel him. First he must ask him to leave and give him sufficient time and reasonable opportunity to depart peacefully. If the trespasser does not leave as requested then the owner, or another person on his instructions, may use reasonable force to make him leave. What is "reasonable" force in general terms can be a difficult question to answer.

Apart from the question of trespass anyone who is assaulted or manhandled by another may sue him for assault and/or battery whether he is actually injured or not. An assault takes place when one person aims a blow at another, or attempts to grasp him, or makes a threatening gesture, especially if he were to point a gun at him. A battery occurs when the person is either struck or grasped or even touched. However if the person grasped or threatened is a trespasser, then the owner of the land, or someone acting on his instructions, who lays hands upon him to expel him has a good defence to an action for assault and battery, provided that he does not exceed what is reasonable force in the circumstances. A peaceful trespasser may be pushed, or grasped by the arm and

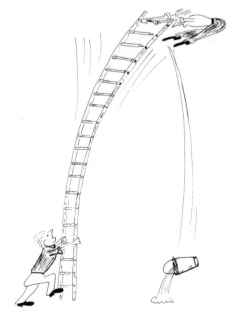

He gently shook the ladder and gently turned it over and gently threw the plaintiff from it upon the ground.

propelled towards the exit but the owner must not beat him, wound him or do anything else to injure him. A defendant in an assault case, who claimed that the injured man was trespassing, when climbing a ladder, and had refused to leave, said that he "gently shook the ladder and gently overturned it and gently threw the Plaintiff from it upon the ground, thereby doing as little damage as possible to the Plaintiff". The court decided he had not been gentle enough, and the force was not justified. Also an owner must be careful that in ejecting the trespasser he does not expose him to serious risk of physical injury, even though he does not injure him directly. He could not, for example, push the trespasser off his land into a river, or force him to jump off a high wall. In one case the court held that the owner was liable for turning out a sick trespasser into the snow. It is, however, a different story if the trespasser offers violence to the owner, or tries to make a forcible entry into his property.

An owner who is assaulted or physically threatened by a trespasser is entitled to defend himself and the rules of self defence then apply. A person defending himself, or someone else, from an attack is entitled to use much more force than someone expelling a peaceful trespasser. He is not obliged to wait for a blow to be struck against him, but may strike first. Even so the amount of force used must not be greater than is reasonable. There are some interesting old cases in which the rules were explained, for instance: "if A strikes B, B cannot justify the drawing of his sword and cutting off A's hand". But ideas of what is permissible force in the case of an assault change with time. A leading English judge once said that "if an author is to go and give a beating to a publisher who has offended him, two or three blows with a horse whip ought to be quite sufficient to satisfy his irritated feelings", but such action would obviously not be tolerated nowadays. However it was stated in a more modern case that "if you are attacked with a deadly weapon you can defend yourself with a deadly weapon or any other weapon which may protect your life. The law does not concern itself with niceties in such cases. If you are attacked by a prize-fighter you are not bound to adhere to the Queensbury Rules in your defence".

There is also a difference between the action a landowner may take to defend his property against possible trespassers, and the action he may take against a trespasser actually on the land. He may deter people from entering by fixing broken glass to the top of his walls, or iron spikes to his railings. An intruder who impales himself on such spikes cannot complain, but the owner cannot thrust an iron spike into a trespasser. Similarly he may keep savage guard dogs in his grounds, provided some warning of their presence is given, but he must not set the dogs upon a trespasser he finds in his garden. Even so there are limits to how far the homeowner can go in defending his property. Highly dangerous defensive measures such as spring guns, mantraps and high voltage electric fences would not be permitted. Although fierce dogs may be kept in the grounds, the keeping of animals such as lions or poisonous snakes for protection is not allowed.

4. Burglars

The laws regarding the defence of one's home and family against burglars and other criminals are basically the same as those governing self help against trespassers and self defence against assault. The homeowner who finds a burglar in his house may arrest him and hold him until the police come. He may *not* shoot him out of hand. However if the burglar resists arrest, or assaults him, the homeowner may use reasonable force to protect himself and to detain the burglar.

A homeowner in dealing with a burglar is far more likely to use violence than he would in dealing with a casual trespasser. He must remember however that there is not only the possibility of a private action for assault (perhaps unlikely in the case of a burglar caught in the act) but that he may be prosecuted by the police if he really injures the man. If he were to kill or seriously injure the burglar there would certainly be a strong probability of a criminal prosecution, unless he clearly acted in self defence of himself or his family whose own lives were threatened.

In practice the law is likely to deal leniently with a person who uses violence against a burglar, kidnapper, or other criminal who has invaded his house, provided that he does not go too far. If he were to be prosecuted and pleaded self defence, a jury would be unlikely to find him guilty if he acted in the heat of the moment and provided that he had not obviously used excessive violence in the circumstances. What would *not* be tolerated, however, would be any violent act against a burglar who was already disabled, or who had surrendered peacefully, or who was held down or tied up. No matter how outraged the homeowner may feel about the violation of his home he must not give way to a desire for revenge.

5. Persons lawfully on the land

Naturally there is no trespass by a person who is lawfully upon the land. This includes people who themselves have a legal right to the property, people to whom the law gives a right of entry, and people invited in by the owner or given permission by him to be there.

When a property is jointly owned each owner has an absolute right of occupation and entry unless it is let to a tenant. The wife or husband of an owner has the right to enter and occupy the matrimonial home unless there has been a legal separation or a court has made an order excluding her or him from the property. As mentioned in Chapter 1 it is possible that a joint owner, or even an absolute owner, may be excluded from the house by a court order, but an entry made in contravention of such an order would not be trespass but simply a breach of the order.

A tenant has as much right of occupation as any other owner, and in fact a landlord may be a trespasser upon his own property if he enters it without the tenant's consent. However an owner who takes in lodgers is not trespassing when he enters a lodger's room. Indeed one of the tests applied to decide whether someone who occupies a room is a tenant or a lodger is "does the occupier have the right to exclude the owner of the property?"

No-one who enters property at the invitation, or with the consent of the owner is a trespasser so long as the consent continues. However he will become a trespasser if he stays on the property too long where the consent is for a specific length of time, or if he fails to leave when the owner withdraws his consent. This does not mean he becomes a trespasser as soon as the owner says those words so familiar to lovers of Westerns, "get off my land!" He must be allowed reasonable time to leave and to remove his goods or possessions from the property. The difference between his position and that of the trespasser who enters the property without consent is that the trespasser must be given reasonable time to leave before he can be forcibly ejected, but can still be sued for trespass; the person who entered with consent cannot be sued provided that he leaves within a reasonable time of being told to go.

There is a general assumption that anyone approaching the front of a house by walking up a drive or path from the road has the owner's consent to be there. If this were not so no-one could call at a house set back from the road without being a trespasser. Of course the same rules apply to such a visitor as apply to anyone invited to the house by the owner; he will become a trespasser once ordered to leave the land and given sufficient time to remove himself and his belongings. However such a person may be given orders by the owner never to darken his door again, in which case any entry by him will be a trespass unless he is specifically invited to return. But the owner may give a warning to the public in general, or to a particular section, that he wants no-one to enter without explicit invitation. He can achieve this by posting notices around his land saying "No entry" followed no doubt by the time honoured but untrue statement "Trespassers will be prosecuted" which will warn everyone to keep out. A notice saying "No hawkers" will be regarded as sufficient to keep out door to door salesmen.

There are many cases in which the person enters the property not just with the owner's consent but because he has a contract with him. In the case of the owner engaging a decorator or a plumber to do some work for him then consent to come onto the property must be included. In such a case the owner is obliged by his agreement to allow the contractor to stay until the work is done, but he does not lose the right to control the use of his property. He is still able to order the contractor to leave the land if he does not like the way the work is being done, or for any other reason, however trivial. The contractor may be entitled to claim compensation for breach of contract, and may even succeed in obtaining full payment for the work which he was prevented from doing by the owner's unreasonable behaviour. Nevertheless he must leave when requested to do so and will become a trespasser if he refuses.

The position may be different if someone pays for entry to the property or for something which necessitates his entering. For example someone who has paid for a seat at a theatre does not become a trespasser if the owner asks him to leave unless there is very good reason. This will not normally concern the ordinary homeowner but it is possible that he may take in a paying lodger, or may accept payment for allowing a football match to be played on his field at the back of his house, or may charge people an entrance fee for a cheese and wine party in aid of charity. In such a case he must remember that he cannot simply order someone to leave. If he should use force to expel such a person he may be sued for assault and would not be able to plead that he was ejecting a trespasser. Of course, the person must behave in a proper orderly manner and comply with any conditions agreed between them. A paying visitor who started a fight, painted graffiti on the wall, or pocketed the silver cutlery, could certainly be ordered to leave and would become a trespasser if he refused.

There are certain people who are authorised by the law to enter the property of another even without his consent. Such obvious examples as firemen fighting a fire spring to mind. Also legal rights for a landlord or a court bailiff to distrain for rent (i.e. take goods in payment) prevent their entry being a trespass. Policemen may enter property to prevent a crime or to arrest a criminal caught in the act, or one for whom a warrant has been issued. In one case the court decided that even a private person did not commit trespass when he broke into a house to prevent the owner from murdering his wife. But once more these exceptions to the law of trespass will be lost if the person entering the property does not behave in a strictly correct manner, and the policeman, bailiff or landlord who exceeds his powers may become a trespasser.

Anyone using rights of way and other rights over private land is not trespassing. This is so whether the right is a public right of way over a public footpath, a private right of way over a joint drive or, for example, a right to go onto the property next door to carry out repairs to the wall of one's house. The important thing to remember is that the person exercising the right may be lawfully on another's land, but only so long as he is doing what is permitted. He must keep to the roadway or path and not stray onto the land adjoining it. He must not use it as a racetrack, block it by parking vehicles, or carry on any other activities not covered by the right granted to him. If he does things which go beyond the reasonable use of the right then he may become a trespasser.

It is even possible that a person using a public highway may become a trespasser. There are many houses built next to roads, in both town and country, whose owners have a legal title not only to the house and garden but also to the section of road adjoining it. Usually in such cases the plans on the deeds show the ownership extending to the centre of the road. In those cases the homeowners own the land on which that part of the road is built although the highway authority owns the surface of the road and the public have the right to use it. It is probable that the only real advantage of this arrangement to the homeowner is that anyone who behaves in an improper manner on the road outside the house may become a trespasser. This was illustrated by the case of a racehorse owner who sued a racing tout for trespass. The tout had walked up and down a fifteen yard stretch of road observing the horses training on the adjoining land and making notes about their form. The court held that he had trespassed on the racehorse owner's land which extended under the road.

6. Safety of premises and injury to people who enter them

In days gone by the responsibility of the occupier of property for the safety of people who came on his land or into his buildings was rather complicated. There were some fine distinctions drawn between people who were there on business, or as guests, or merely on sufferance, or as trespassers. Many of the difficulties were removed by the Occupiers' Liability Act 1957, but even now the legal rules are not entirely straightforward.

People entering the property of another are now placed in two basic categories: those who have a lawful right to be on the land, and those who have not. The people having a lawful right include all those who are there at the invitation of the occupier or with his permission and also people to whom the law gives rights of entry such as firemen fighting a fire, policemen with a warrant and landlords distraining for rent. The occupier has a duty "to take such care as in all the circumstances of the case is reasonable to see that the visitor will be reasonably safe in using the premises for the purpose for which he is invited or permitted to be there". This means that any visitor who is injured, or whose belongings are damaged, because of some fault or usual danger on the property, will generally be entitled to compensation from the occupier. However, the defect or danger has to be something that the occupier knows about, or which he ought to know about. He will not be liable for damages if the injury was caused by something which he did not know about, unless it was something which a normally prudent person could have expected or would have noticed if he had looked. The owner for example might not be liable to a visitor who is injured by an explosion caused by a gas leak about which the owner knew nothing, but if there had been a strong smell of gas in the house for several days and he had not bothered to have it investigated then he could be held responsible.

The owner or occupier who knows that there is something dangerous on the property must make sure that no-one who comes into it is injured. If he cannot remove the source of danger, or shield or otherwise protect visitors from it, then he must give them clear and adequate warning about it. He must also remember that children are at a greater risk of injury than adults because they are more likely to go poking into out of the way corners of the property, and less likely to recognise the danger when they find it. The duty to protect and warn children is that much stronger on account of this. And even when someone has been fully warned about the danger there are circumstances in which he may get compensation from the owner if he acts in a reasonable way. For example a visitor who is injured whilst rescuing someone else from a danger that he knows all about may still be entitled to damages.

Even so there are cases in which the owner or occupier may not himself be liable for injury to a visitor. If the visitor is injured because of faulty workmanship by an independent contractor employed by the owner then it is usually the contractor who must pay the compensation. And when the injured person is himself a contractor, called in as an expert to deal with a particular problem, the owner will not normally be liable if he is injured by the very thing he has been employed to deal with. An electrician who is electrocuted by faulty wiring, or a chimney sweep overcome by poisonous fumes in a chimney, cannot normally claim compensation. But if it is the electrician who is overcome by the poisonous fumes then he will have the same right to claim damages as anyone else lawfully on the premises.

Now we come to the other category, people who are not lawfully on the premises. At one time the law was quite harsh in its treatment of trespassers who, it was said "must take the land as they find it". This absolved the owner or occupier from any responsibility for injury to the trespasser or his belongings except for action deliberately intended to harm the trespasser. While the occupier could not set spring guns on his land or keep savage beasts there without adequate security precautions, he was under no duty to protect a trespasser from other dangers such as half hidden pits in the ground, dangerous machinery, high voltage electric wires or a staircase riddled with dry rot. But the occupier/owner is no longer let off so lightly.

During recent years the courts have evolved a new and more humane approach to the problem. This may be summarised by saying that the occupier must act in accordance with common standards of civilised behaviour and humanity. One senior judge in an appeal before the House of Lords described the occupier as "owing a duty of care to the trespasser if a reasonable man, knowing only the physical facts which the occupier actually knew, would appreciate that a trespasser's presence at the point and time of danger was so likely that in all the circumstances it would be inhumane not to give him effective warning of the danger". Other judges have gone further saying that the occupier is responsible if there is a stong possibility of a trespass.

Once more the law draws a distinction between adults and children. Because children are more likely to stray into forbidden territory, and more likely to be attracted by dangers such as fires, water or machinery, the occupier must take more care to prevent injury to them. Warning notices are rarely sufficient and walls or fences to keep them away from the danger may be necessary.

The distinction between a trespasser and someone lawfully upon the land can sometimes be difficult to draw. As mentioned earlier a person who approaches a house by walking from the road up the front driveway is usually asssumed by the law to have the implied consent of the owner to be there. He is therefore not a trespasser. But the law goes further than this. An occupier or owner who turns a blind eye to trespassers who regularly cross or enter his land may be treated as having given them consent by implication. Even when the owner has protested against the trespassers entering his land and told them not to do so again, he may be treated as giving implied consent if he then does nothing further to stop their entry when they keep doing it. Again the responsibility to children is greater than to adults and to avoid his responsibility the owner must take really firm steps to keep them out.

Fortunately for most homeowners their household or other insurance policies usually cover the risk of an action for damages by someone injured on the premises. Anyone who is doubtful about this should certainly check his insurance policies to make sure that one of them does give him protection. As will have been noted the homeowner is frequently at risk of an action for damages by someone injured even though he might not know that they are on his property, or that a particular danger exists. The compensation awarded by the courts to a person suffering serious injury can be very high indeed.

7. Damage to neighbouring property or passers-by

Most actions for damages which come before the courts are based on negligence. The meaning of negligence is fairly obvious and easy for anyone to understand. A person who acts carelessly or recklessly is being negligent and anyone who is injured by such action has a right to sue for damages. When the injury occurs upon someone else's property the injured person can obtain damages against the person whose negligence caused the injury, whether it was the owner of the property, the occupier, or anyone else who just happened to be there. This is quite separate from the right to obtain damages from the owner or occupier because the property itself was dangerous or contained dangerous things as mentioned in section 6 of this chapter. But of course the negligence might not all be on one side. The person injured may himself have contributed to the accident by his own negligence and in that case the court has to apportion the blame between them, and apportion the compensation awarded accordingly.

The same principle applies to someone outside the property who is injured, or suffers damage to his own property or belongings because of the carelessness of someone inside. A person walking down the road who is injured by something dropped from a window above him can sue the occupier for damages. The occupier could only escape liability if he could prove that there had in fact been no negligence and that the injury had resulted from a pure accident for which no-one could be held to blame. Of course the occupier may be able to shift the responsibility to someone else if he can show that they, not he, were responsible for the injury. However, he might still be liable to pay damages if the person who caused the trouble were his employee or perhaps a child under his control.

Closely allied to this responsibility for negligent acts, and sometimes interchangeable with it, is another aspect of the law of nuisance previously mentioned in Chapter 6. The passer-by who is injured by a shutter falling from a building, or the neighbour whose property is damaged by a tree which collapses onto it may be able to obtain compensation. In such cases the owner or occupier will be responsible if he knew or should have known that the shutter's hinges had rusted through, or that the tree was in a dangerous condition. If the owner/occupier can show that the defect was not known by him and could not have been discovered by any reasonably careful inspection then he will have a good defence. For example in the case of a falling tree caused by a disease to the tree roots which could not be observed above ground the owner was held not to be liable. Also if the trouble had been caused by another person or an "Act of God" the owner can be relieved of responsibility. For example if the shutter had fallen because, unknown to the owner, a trespasser had removed the screws from the hinges, or the tree had fallen only as the result of a violent storm, the owner would not have been liable for damages.

There is yet another basis for a claim against the owner of a property when damage occurs to neighbouring premises. This applies when something escapes from the property and causes damage or injury. The rule of law was stated in the leading case as follows: "A person who for his own purpose brings upon his land and collects and keeps there anything likely to do mischief if it escapes must keep it in at his peril".

This strict liability applies to things kept or collected on the land which are not "naturally" there. It has been held to apply to water escaping from a man made lake, oil escaping from a tank, poisonous fumes from a chimney, a "Chairo-plane" which broke loose from a fairground machine, and even such things as poisonous plants, and fire. The difference between claims under this heading and claims under the heading of nuisance is that the claimant does not have to prove that anyone is to blame for the escape. The simple facts that something potentially dangerous was kept or collected on the land, that it escaped, and that it caused injury to people or property are sufficient.

As in the case of claims under the heading of nuisance or negligence there are certain defences available to the landowner. The escape may have been caused by a trespasser or some other person not under the control of the owner. It may have been caused by an Act of God such as a lightning strike, a hurricane force wind, or prolonged torrential rain. The person injured may have consented to the dangerous thing being kept on the land or may himself have been responsible for the escape. Any of these facts may free the landowner wholly or partly from his responsibility.

13

A business in the home

1. Working at home

There is nothing basically wrong with working at home. Many thousands, probably hundreds of thousands, of people in this country work at home from time to time in connection with their jobs or professions, mostly by bringing home paper-work. This is generally regarded as a normal part of everyday living and a proper use of the home. The fact that the homeowner may set aside a room in the house, calling it his "study" or his "office", in which to do this work and in which to keep his papers and books will not of itself prevent that room from being part of the house.

In addition to such casual use of the home for work there are many thousands of people who carry on either a full time or part time business in the home, or operating from the home. There are vast numbers of such businesses capable of being carried on from home, ranging from what is basically a spare time hobby, producing a little extra income, to the transformation of the house into a full time commercial operation. On the one hand the homeowner may paint water colours which he sometimes sells, while on the other he may convert his whole house into a guest house or an old people's home. Depending upon the nature and intensity of any such business operation the effects upon the homeowner may be insignificant, but could be substantial and have serious consequences for him if they should be overlooked.

Whether any particular business use will fall into one category or the other may sometimes be difficult to determine. The various aspects which should be considered are mentioned briefly in this chapter, but anyone proposing to set up a business in the home would be wise to begin by taking professional advice from a solicitor, an accountant, and, if he has no business experience already, the Small Businesses Advisory Council.

2. Planning restrictions

Planning consent is required for any material change of use of the property as was mentioned in Chapter 8. Obviously the conversion of a house into a hotel, guest house, nursing home, shop, offices, etc. will be a material change, and planning consent will have to be obtained even though no physical alteration to the property is envisaged. Similarly a change of use of part of a house, or of an outbuilding to a house, may well require planning consent if it is a material change. But if the use is only casual, or occasional, or insignificant, then this is not regarded as a material change and planning consent will not be necessary.

There are many businesses which can be carried on from the home which do not have any significant effect upon the property. For example someone may carry on business as an insurance agent, either part time or full time, doing his paper-work at home, but going out to see his clients. Although he is certainly carrying on a business from home, and his house is his business address, he is unlikely to be making any material change to any part of the house. Similarly an author may write his books at home, a composer may write his music, or a model maker may make model railway engines which he sells. In all of these cases a material change of use is most unlikely even though a room in the house is used as a study, or music room, or a garage is used for the model making. Such uses of the room or garage would be acceptable as normal domestic uses, and the fact that the owner happens to be making an income from the activity does not appear to be relevant.

Where then does one draw the line between a material change of use of part of the house and an insignificant one? Regrettably, as in many other spheres of the law, it is difficult to give a precise answer to such a general question. Clearly when one room is turned into a shop with goods displayed and the public invited to enter and buy them there is material change of use of that room, and planning permission must be obtained. When a doctor or dentist turns a room in his house into a surgery and treats his patients there, or a hairdresser turns a room into a salon to which customers come for hair styling, there is generally a material change of use. If an accountant turns part of his house into an office and employs a clerk and a secretary who work there each day with him this is likely to be a material change of use of those rooms even though no clients actually come to the house to see him. But how about a music teacher who takes pupils at home where she gives them music lessons in her lounge, or the author who employs a secretary who comes to his house every day to type his work in his study? At what stage does the car enthusiast who restores vintage or classic cars in his garage make a material change of use from a private motor garage to a motor repair shop? And when does the homeowner who takes in lodgers reach the point at which there is a material change of use from a private house to a lodging house or guest house?

Each case has to be decided on its own particular facts. If there should be a disagreement between the homeowner, who maintains that his activities do not amount to a material change in the use of the house, and the local planning authority, who says that they do, and who objects to that use, then the courts would have to make the decision. Among the questions which the court would ask in order to come to a decision would be:-

(a) Are the rooms or the buildings used exclusively for business purposes or partly for business and partly for ordinary domestic purposes?

(b) What is the intensity of the business use: for how many hours per week does it continue?

(c) Are other people employed to work there: if so how many and on how regular a basis?

(d) Do customers call at the house: how many and how often?

(e) Does the activity affect the neighbours, as by creating noise, fumes, vibrations etc., or by substantially increasing the traffic in the road?

3. Restrictions in the deeds

Many houses in this country, and virtually all residential flats or apartments, are affected by restrictions of some kind contained in their deeds controlling the use of the property for business purposes. These range from covenants providing a blanket exclusion such as "not to carry on upon the premises any trade, business or profession whatsoever"; to covenants which prohibit specific business

Do customers call at the house? How many and how often?

activities such as "not to sell upon the premises any beers, wines or spiritous liquors".

In the last century deeds of conveyance of building land frequently prohibited "obnoxious or objectionable" businesses and usually listed a large number of specific businesses which would not be permitted such as "tallow chandler, soap boiler, tanner, copper smelter, slaughterhouse" and so on. In more recent times when restrictions have been imposed on the sale of houses in a new building estate they have tended to be in wider terms prohibiting any business use except perhaps certain professions such as a doctor or solicitor, or simply saying that "the property shall not be used for any purpose other than as a private dwelling-house with the usual outbuildings". In most cases all these restrictions are still in force.

Anyone considering beginning a business in a private house should certainly check that the deeds do not contain covenants which could be used to prevent him from operating. Such covenants, if they exist and are still enforceable, could conceivably cause him a great deal more trouble than the planning laws. If a proposed business use is clearly in contravention of the covenants then unless the people entitled to the benefit will agree to modify the covenants or to release the homeowner from them, they may well foil his plans completely. Failing agreement the only possible way out for the would-be entrepreneur is an application to the court for an order discharging the covenant on the ground that the nature of the district has changed so much that the covenant is no longer relevant.

A restrictive covenant may prohibit the homeowner from carrying on a business for which he has obtained planning permission. It may even prevent him from carrying on a business for which no planning permission would have been necessary because the operation of the business would not result in a material change being made in the use of the property. For example a music teacher giving singing lessons or violin lessons in the lounge may not have made a material change of use for which planning consent would have been required. However he is still carrying on his business or profession. If the next door neighbour has the benefit of a covenant that no trade, business, or profession shall be carried on in the teacher's house, and the noise is disturbing him, then he may be able to apply to the court for an injunction to stop the teacher from giving lessons at home.

Whether a covenant will be effective to prevent a particular use of the property is dependent on a number of things. The following questions must be considered:-

(a) Does the wording of the covenant prohibit the use in question? A covenant which prohibits certain named uses, or "obnoxious" or "objectionable" businesses, will not prevent the owner from carrying on some other quite unobjectionable trade or business. It has been held that words prohibiting the owner from carrying on a "trade or business" will not prevent him from carrying on a "learned profession".

(b) Does the breach of covenant have a detrimental effect upon the neighbours who might wish to enforce it?

(c) Has the covenant lapsed because the person or persons entitled to the benefit have allowed the owner to carry on the business in breach of the covenant for a long period without trying to take any action to prevent him?

(d) Has the nature of the district changed to such an extent that the covenant is no longer relevant and is therefore likely to be discharged by the court?

If the particular business will be a breach of a covenant which is still enforceable then the owner should try to obtain a release from it. He may well be asked to pay for the release of the covenant, and if the person who now has the benefit of the covenant sees an opportunity to exact a large sum out of him then it could be costly. The biggest problem, however, may be in tracing the people who now have the benefit of the covenant and can release it.

In the case of leaseholds there is less likely to be a problem than with freeholds. The lessor, being the person who is now entitled to the freehold interest in the property, will be collecting the ground rent so his identity will be known. The leasehold tenant will have no difficulty in contacting him to request a release from the covenants contained in the original lease. But even with leasehold property there may be difficulties if the freehold was itself subject to restrictive covenants even before the lease was granted. In that case it is likely that there may still be other property in the vicinity to which the benefit of the covenants is attached so that consent must also be sought from the owners of that neighbouring property.

With covenants on freeholds the difficulty often lies in identifying the persons who are now entitled to enforce the covenant. If the covenants were imposed fairly recently then the right to enforce them will probably still lie with the people to whom they were originally granted. In the case of older covenants, and this usually but not always means those on older properties, the benefit may have changed hands several times. How then does one decide whom one should approach to request a release?

There are two basic aspects to a covenant: firstly it is a personal promise made by one person to another; but secondly it is a restriction attached to the land. So far as the personal promise is concerned the person who makes it must always honour it so long as he and the covenantee (i.e. the person to whom he made it) are both alive. If he fails then the covenantee can take action in the courts against him. Even when he has parted with the land he may be sued for damages if the promise is broken by the new owner of the land. For this reason it is usual for anyone buying land subject to an existing covenant to give a new covenant to the vendor promising to observe and perform the covenants and to protect him from any claim which may be made against him because of any future breach of the covenants. Although the new owner does not himself owe any personal responsibility to the original covenantee, he may possibly be attacked in a roundabout way by the original covenantee suing the person who originally gave the covenant and who in turn sues the person who bought the land from him and who promised to indemnify him. This method of enforcement can be used whether the covenant is a restrictive one or a positive one. But once either of the original parties, or any intermediate owner, has died, the chain breaks.

The second aspect is the restriction attached to the land. Provided that the proper procedures have been followed to protect this restriction it will apply to anyone who buys the property. However, because this is a restriction attached to land, the benefit must also be attached to land. It is the present owner of the neighbouring land to which the benefit is attached who has the right to enforce the covenant against the property and its present owner. But whoever tries to enforce the covenant in this way must prove that the benefit of the covenant has passed to him. He may do this either by showing that the benefit of the covenant was transferred to him when he bought the land which benefits from the covenant, or that when the covenant was created it was specifically attached to the piece of land which he has now purchased.

Before any terms are agreed for the release of a covenant, and certainly before any payment is made, the homeowner must be quite sure that it is not only the right person, but also the only person entitled to the covenant who is now releasing it. This is obviously a task which he should entrust to his solicitors. They will have to make detailed research into the covenants and the history of the various properties to establish who exactly can now claim to have the benefit of the covenants. Both the research and the payments eventually demanded for the release of the covenants may well prove to be expensive.

Even though the homeowner may be prepared to pay a substantial sum for the release of the covenants there is no guarantee that they will be released. The control of the environment is often of more concern to the neighbouring owners than any financial gain which they might make from granting the required release. It is something which anyone thinking of purchasing a house with a view to carrying on a business there, either now or later, should keep firmly in mind. If the property which he wishes to buy has a covenant affecting it which could prevent him from running his business there he should investigate the situation now, whether he is also applying for planning consent or not. If it appears that the covenants are likely to present a problem then he should seriously reconsider his proposed purchase before he is committed to a contract.

4. Other problems affecting particular businesses

There are certain businesses which are subject to additional controls. As it happens a number of these are just the kind of business which the owner of a large house may wish to run at his home. They include using the house as a hotel, a restaurant, a nursing home, an old people's home, or a school.

If alcoholic drinks are to be provided at a restaurant or hotel the proprietor, or manager, who runs it must obtain a licence from the local magistrates. If a new restaurant or hotel is to be opened the first hurdle to be overcome by the owner who wishes to obtain a licence is that the magistrates must be convinced that the grant of a new licence is justifiable. In an area already well equipped with hotels and restaurants they may refuse to grant any new licences. Indeed it is generally difficult to obtain any new licence for the sale of alcohol throughout the country, and a very good case has to be presented to persuade the magistrates that a licensed restaurant or hotel is desirable in that particular location.

Assuming that the magistrates are prepared to grant a licence for the premises, the second hurdle is to satisfy them that the owner is a suitable person to hold the licence. Any applicant must satisfy the magistrates that he is of good character and is capable of running a licensed establishment in a proper orderly manner. The police will be required to report upon his background and to state whether they have any objections to him as a licensee. If they oppose his application he will almost certainly not be granted the licence. The other information which the magistrates will want is about his previous employment and particularly his experience in the licensed trade. The chances of anyone with no relevant experience obtaining a new licence for premises which he wishes to convert are remote indeed.

In the case of the homeowner wishing to convert his house into a private nursing home, an old people's home, or a school, a licence is usually required from the local authority. When anyone applies for planning consent to convert a house and use it for one of these businesses the planning department refer the application to a number of other departments so that reports may be made, not only about the suitability of the property for the proposed use, but also as to the suitability of the owner to carry on the business. In the case of a nursing home or old people's home the health department is consulted. In the case of a proposed school the education department will be interested. In the case of any proposed change of use which will mean that the property will be regularly occupied or used by a large number of people, the fire department will make recommendation about fire escapes and the general fitness of the property. And it is not only the fitness of the property, but also the desirability of having an increased number of such establishments in the area, upon which the decision will be made.

5. Outgoings and taxation

If a house, part of a house, or its outbuildings are converted to a business use there is likely to be an increase in the general rates and water rates. Business rates rather than domestic rates will be charged on the part used for the business which will be separately assessed. Of course there will be a corresponding reduction in the domestic rates which will then be charged on part only of the former house. There may also be an alteration in the electricity and gas accounts with the business part of the premises being separately metred and the supplies charged at the different rates applicable to domestic use and small commercial use.

When the rates and other outgoings are split in this way the owner has the opportunity to claim tax relief on the business expenditure. The fact that the business premises are separately rated provides evidence that the expenditure is for business purposes.

It is also possible that someone operating his business from home may obtain tax relief even though no part of the house is separately rated as business premises. If he can show that he does conduct his business from home then the Inland Revenue will usually accept that a proportion of the outgoings of the premises are business expenses, and allow him to deduct that proportion from his business profits when he calculates his income for tax purposes. However the homeowner who does some work at home should be wary of making such a claim because it might affect the relief which he will be allowed from capital gains tax when he eventually sells the house (see Chapter 14).

Taxation and the home

1. Taxation of the homeowner

The homeowner is affected by our tax system in a number of ways. He may have to pay income tax on profits made by him out of the property, but relief from income tax is often available on his mortgage interest payments. Capital gains tax may be payable on the gain made when he sells, but relief is given to him on the gain made on the sale of his principal residence. Inheritance tax may be payable on property passing to him under a Will or intestacy, and until recently could become payable when property was given to him as a gift. Also recently abolished was development land tax, the latest of a number of taxes or other measures designed to take away from the individual the benefit, or a large part of the benefit, of any increase in value of his property arising out of its potential for development. However there are certain circumstances in which he might even become liable to pay VAT on the profit made from a letting.

The first consideration for many homeowners is the relief which might be available on mortgage interest payments. This has already been covered in Chapter 10. But the homeowner should always remember that any profit he makes from his property, whether it is rent from a short term letting, an annual payment for the use of a temporary right of way, an occasional hiring of part of his land for some recreational use, or any other profit made by him, is income which must be shown in his annual tax return. Failure to do this would be a breach of the tax laws and could have serious consequences.

Capital gains tax can be of even more concern to the homeowner, as it may take away a large slice of the money he receives on a sale unless he is entitled to relief from it. Fortunately for the homeowner there is relief from this tax on the sale of his principal residence and in certain other cases. This chapter is principally about the effect of capital gains tax, although some reference is made to the effect of income tax, and other taxes, in certain special cases.

As mentioned above the taxes formerly charged on gifts, and on development value, have recently been abolished; although it is likely that from time to time, with changing governments, these old taxes will be re-introduced or replaced with something similar. Inheritance tax is just the latest in a long history of taxes charged upon property passing on a death; it is really outside the scope of this book.

2. Capital gains tax – private residence exemption

To the average homeowner the most important exemption from liability for capital gains tax (CGT) is that which applies to his home. Being his most valuable asset it is also the one on which he is likely to make a substantial gain when he sells it. Of course the gain is normally on paper only as capital gains generally reflect the effect of inflation rather than any genuine increase in the value of the asset. If the gain upon a house were not exempt from this tax it would make moving house very difficult for most homeowners, who usually put into the new house which they are buying virtually all the money received on the sale of the old one.

The exemption applies to the principal private residence. If the homeowner is lucky enough to own a second home, be it a seaside chalet, a country cottage, a flat in the city, or even a large caravan on a permanent site, he must decide which is his principal residence on which the tax exemption is to be claimed. Normally he will, of course, choose the property on which the best gain is likely to be made. Provided that he gives written notice to the Inspector of Taxes stating which of the two homes is to be regarded as his principal residence, then that property will be exempt from CGT when he sells it. The notice, which is called an election, may be given at any time within two years of the homeowner becoming the owner of the two properties, but if no election is made within that time the Inspector of Taxes will make the decision as to which of the two properties actually is the principal residence. Although the homeowner has a right of appeal against that decision if he does not agree with it, the Inspector's conclusion will probably be upheld, so it is obviously best to avoid this problem by making the election within the time allowed. If the properties, or either of them, are jointly owned by a husband and wife, or if the husband owns one and the wife owns the other, they must both sign the election notice for it to be valid. Should they disagree about which property to choose, or if for some reason one of them fails to sign the election, then again the Tax Inspector will make the decision for them.

When a property has been occupied by the homeowner as his principal residence for only part of the time during which he has owned it, any gain he makes is apportioned on a time basis. This can happen in a variety of ways. For example a property may be used by the owner as a private residence for part of the period of his ownership, and as his place of business during the rest of the time. Alternatively it may have been let to a tenant for part of the period (but it should be noted that special rules now apply in the case of a letting to a residential tenant which have the effect of reducing the tax payable). Then, of course, it may have ceased to be his principal residence because he has elected for another property to be the principal residence. In any of these cases the increase in value when the home is sold or transferred is divided between the time when it was his principal residence, and the period when it was not. In calculating the gain an allowance is also given for any money spent on extending or improving the property, and the costs incurred in buying and selling it. A further allowance is now available in most cases to take into account the effect of inflation since March 1982, although no account is taken of the effect of inflation before that date.

Capital gains tax is charged upon the increase in value of an asset when the owner disposes of it. It is not necessary for the asset to be sold for the tax to be charged, and there need be no gain made by the owner. The tax is charged when he gives the asset away, and a valuation must then be made to assess the notional "gain" on which the tax is based. If he sells it at a price below its true value then the same rules apply and a notional "gain" is calculated on the full value of the asset at that time. Sometimes it is necessary for the owner who sells to prove that it was a genuine sale and that he got the best price which he could. It must therefore be remembered that whenever a property is subject to a charge of CGT, whether it is chargeable on the whole property or only on a part, then any gift of the property, or any sale to a friend or relative at a reduced price, will give rise to a charge to the tax, which has to be paid by the person selling or giving away the property, not by the person who receives it. Between husband and wife, however, no transfer of an asset gives rise to a charge to CGT because for the purpose of this tax they are treated as being one person.

As an example of how these rules operate imagine the case of Mr Jones who in 1966 bought for £6,000 a house occupied by a business tenant who used it as offices. In 1969 the tenant left, and Mr & Mrs Jones then lived in the house themselves. Three years later Jones bought a flat in London where he lived during the week, returning each weekend to the house where his wife lived all the time. He elected for the flat to be his principal residence, so when he sold it five years later the gain on the flat was exempt from CGT but during those five years the house lost its exemption from the tax. After selling the flat Jones spent £7,500 on an extension to the house, where he and his wife continued to live until he sold it in 1986 for £96,000. The cost of selling (estate agents' commission and legal fees), together with the costs when he purchased it, amounted to £2,500. His gain to be taxed is calculated as follows:-

Sale price of house		£96,000

Deduct the following:-

Purchase price	6,000	
Cost of extension	7,500	
Costs of purchase and sale	2,500	
	16,000	16,000
Net increase in value		£80,000

Periods for which NO exemption
is granted:

Tenant's occupation	3 years
Period during which the flat was the principal residence	5 years
Total period for which tax is to be charged	8 years

Total period of ownership	20 years

$$\text{Taxable gain is} \quad \frac{80,000 \times 8 \text{ (years)}}{20 \text{ (years)}} = \qquad £32,000$$

In fact a further allowance would be made to take into account the effect of inflation from March 1982 up to the time of sale which would result in a relatively small reduction in the amount of the taxable gain.

A note of warning must be sounded here. The relief from CGT applying to the gain on the taxpayer's principal residence only applies to a gain made in the normal course of events on the sale of his own house. If anyone buys a house with the intention of making a gain out of it, any gain he makes when he sells will be subject to CGT. It would not normally be easy for the Inland Revenue to prove that someone buying a house for his own occupation had bought it with the intention of making a profit, even though he may well have considered the possibility. For this reason it is rare for claims to be made for tax on this ground. However the homeowner should keep in mind the fact that tax can become payable, on the disposal of his house and should certainly avoid making any statement, especially in writing, that when he bought the house he had expected to make a gain from it.

There is an even worse fate which might befall the poor homeowner who is unwise enough to move house too often. If he buys and sells houses fairly quickly at a profit the Inland Revenue may claim that he is trading in property. When he has bought and sold three times quickly in succession, making a good

If he buys and sells houses fairly quickly at a profit the Inland Revenue may claim that he is trading in property.

profit each time, especially if the houses are all in the same area and there is no particular reason for him to keep moving, then he might find it difficult to deny that he was making a business of it. In that case any gains made would not be subject to CGT, but would be treated as trading profits subject to income tax. The gain made in any tax year would be added to any other income he had in order to assess the rate at which tax would be payable, and he might well be taxed at a much higher rate than the 30% rate charged on capital gains.

3. Selling part of the garden

The exemption from CGT includes the land on which the house stands together with a garden, or other grounds, not exceeding one acre in area. It is in fact possible for an area exceeding an acre to be exempt if the Tax Commissioners are satisfied that the size and character of the house are such that a larger area of garden "is required for the reasonable enjoyment of it as a residence". In practice when a house and its garden are sold it will generally be accepted that the garden is exempt even if it does exceed an acre, within reason of course. The problems usually arise when part of the garden is sold separately.

The relief from CGT, given on a gain arising upon the transfer of a house and its garden is extended to include a gain arising upon the transfer of part of the house or garden. However, when a part of the garden, or other land occupied with the house, is sold it is usually because someone expects, or hopes, to be able to build upon it and offers the homeowner a price which far exceeds the value of the land as a garden. It is hardly surprising that when presented with such a transaction the Inspector of Taxes takes a hard look at it to see whether it is one in which the substantial gain made by the vendor should be exempt from CGT. If the total area of land with the house exceeds one acre, then the homeowner is likely to have a fight upon his hands, and will probably be called upon to present a case to the Commissioners of Taxes in order to satisfy them that no part of the gain should be taxed.

If it is the view of the Commissioners that the total area of the land is too great to be completely exempt, then they must decide which part is free from the tax and which is taxable. They may decide that no more than one acre is exempt, or in a suitable case they could decide that one and a half acres, or two acres, would be a reasonable amount of land for the particular house.

They are then required to make a decision about which part of the land would be most suitable as a garden for the house if the rest were separately occupied. If the land sold is the farthest away from the house it is likely that the gain will be taxable, but if, in the view of the Commissioners, the piece sold is within the part which is most suitable as a garden for the house then it would still be exempt. Of course it often happens that part of the piece of land sold is within the exempt area, while the rest is taxable, and in that case the gain is apportioned between the taxable part and the tax free part.

Unfortunately for the homeowner, the possibility of tax being charged upon a gain made when part of his land is transferred is not only decided upon the area of the land he owns. The exemption is specifically attached to the dwelling-house and "land which he has for his own occupation and enjoyment with that residence as its garden or grounds up to the permitted area". Even if the total land he owns does not exceed one acre, or whatever size is considered reasonable for the house in question, he may not be saved from tax upon it if at the time of the sale he has not been in occupation of it as part of the garden or grounds to the house. Any land, for example, which has been used by him for his business, or which has been let to a local farmer for grazing , will be outside the exemption and will be subject to the tax if sold at a profit.

The homeowner who sees the possibility of selling part of his land at a profit must be wary of how he goes about it. He must *not* sell the house and retain part of the garden to be sold later as building land. If he does so the land he retains ceases to be used as a garden to his house once the house itself has been sold. Any gain made when the piece of land is later sold will be wholly subject to CGT. He should even be careful about taking steps which have the effect of detaching the land to be sold from the rest of his garden before selling it. If he has fenced off part of the garden, then obtained planning permission to build on it before offering it for sale, it may be decided that as he has ceased to use it as part of his garden before selling it the exemption has been lost. The safest policy from his point of view is to agree to sell the land first, then let the intending purchaser apply for planning permission before physically separating it from the rest of his garden. There can then be little doubt that the piece of land sold has remained part of the garden, and therefore subject to the exemption, until sold.

4. Husband and wife

A husband and his wife living with him are treated as one person so far as capital gains tax is concerned. Any gain by one is treated as a gain by them both, and they are jointly taxed as a single person. For the same reason they are allowed only one principal residence between them. Even though the wife owns one property and the husband owns the other they must jointly elect which of the properties is to be their principal residence and therefore exempt from CGT. The fact that the husband lives mainly in one and the wife in the other, as when he lives in his flat in London during the week, while his wife lives all the time in their house in the country to which he returns each weekend, is irrelevant because they are still living together. Only when there is a genuine separation, with each of them establishing a separate household and living completely apart, can both properties be treated as exempt from CGT.

The general rule is that the tax exemption applies only when the owner of a house lives in it himself, but an exception is made in the case of a husband and wife who are separated. When the owner of the house moves out leaving his wife (or her husband in the case of a house legally owned by the wife) in occupation, relief from CGT can still be claimed if the house is eventually transferred to the other spouse (or ex-spouse when they have been divorced) as part of a matrimonial or divorce settlement. This relief, however, applies only when the owner has not in the meantime elected for another property to be his or her principal residence, and provided that the spouse has continued to occupy the former matrimonial home as her, or his, main residence.

Because a husband and his wife living together are treated as one person for the purpose of CGT, no tax becomes payable when one transfers to the other any asset which is subject to a charge to CGT. Any gain which is made on the sale of an asset, which has been previously transferred between the husband and wife, will be assessed according to the price paid when the asset was purchased from an outsider. Again some adjustment is allowed for the effect of inflation after March 1982.

Similar rules apply to relief which a husband and his wife may claim from income tax on mortgage interest, as apply to their relief from CGT. While they are living together tax relief can be claimed in respect of the mortgage interest on one property only, even though they live most of the time in separate properties of which they have separate legal ownership. Only when they are truly separated and living apart all the time can they each claim their own income tax relief on the mortgage interest payments.

5. Trustees, beneficiaries and dependants

For the assessment of CGT on trust property (see the explanation of trusts in Chapter 1), the same relief is available for a gain made on a house or other residence occupied by a beneficiary who is entitled to occupy it under the terms of the trust. A house may perhaps be occupied by a life tenant who has been given a specific right of occupation by the Will which created the trust, and as long as it is the principal residence of the life tenant no tax is charged on any capital gain made by the trustees when they sell it. Even when no absolute right of occupation by a particular beneficiary has been given by the Will or settlement, the exemption still applies when any beneficiary is in occupation with the consent of the trustees, provided that the trustees have been given the power or the discretion to allow the beneficiary to occupy it.

There is a further exemption granted to anyone who provides a home for a dependent relative. It applies to any dwelling-house, or part of a dwelling-house, occupied rent free by a dependent relative of the owner. Such a property is exempt from CGT in addition to the property exempted because it is occupied by the owner himself, but the relief is limited to only one home provided for dependants by any one person (including a married couple). A dependent relative in this case means any relative who is incapacitated by old age or infirmity from maintaining himself, or herself, or the owner's mother or mother-in-law. In the case of the house being provided for the mother or mother-in-law of the owner it is not necessary to show that she is old or infirm but, if not, she must be widowed, divorced, or living apart from her husband.

Income tax relief is also given on mortgage interest paid on a mortgage loan provided for the purpose of buying a house or other residence for a dependent relative. In this case the term "residence" specifically includes a large caravan on a permanent site, or a houseboat. As in the case of exemption from CGT, it is a condition that the residence shall be occupied by the dependant rent free.

6. The owner who is not in residence

Although the general rule is that the homeowner can only claim relief from CGT for a capital gain made during those periods when the house is his principal residence, there are a few exceptions. The first and most important is the period of grace given to him when he has left the property and intends to sell it. Because the sale of a house or flat cannot always be planned to coincide exactly with the owner moving out, he is allowed two years in which to complete the sale after he has left it. Provided that he has lived in the house during part of the period of ownership, he can claim that this last two years be counted as a time when it was his principal residence, whatever the circumstances are at that time.

The second important exception is that the owner may be away from the house for a period during his ownership for any reason. Provided that he was in occupation of the house as his main residence before he went away, that he went back into occupation afterwards, and that no other house was treated as his principal residence during that time, up to three years can be counted as part of the time when it was his principal residence. This three years may be spread over two or more periods of absence. Such absences would not include normal holidays of a few weeks at a time when he would be regarded as still in residence although temporarily out of the house. They would be relevant for example if he went away for a year on a world cruise, letting the house on a temporary tenancy while he was away.

Thirdly he can claim as residence a period during which he is working abroad. There is no restriction on the length of such period abroad, although it is necessary that the employment is wholly outside the United Kingdom.

Lastly he can count any period or periods up to four years in total during which he has worked in any other part of the United Kingdom, or has been obliged to live at his place of work and so has been unable to occupy his own house.

In the last two cases it is again essential that he should have lived in the house after completing his work abroad, or the employment which kept him away from home. However he can have purchased the property ready for his occupation while working abroad, or while working at a job where he was obliged to live in accommodation provided by the employers. Again he may let the house to a tenant during those periods of absence if he wishes. He must not, of course, elect for some other property to be his principal residence during that period of ownership. As the relief from CGT is given separately for each of these reasons it will be noted that it is possible for the owner to be away from the house for many years without becoming liable to pay tax on any part of the gain when he eventually sells it.

7. The second home

There are many homeowners who also own a holiday home or other second home. It may be a house, a flat, or a large caravan on a permanent site. As mentioned earlier in this chapter no relief from CGT will be available unless either the owner elects for it to be his principal home, or it is occupied by someone else whose residence there will qualify for relief. Such other person may be a widowed mother or mother-in-law, or some other dependent relative, or possibly a beneficiary who is entitled to live there under the terms of a trust. Where a member of the owner's family, other than the husband or wife, wishes to live in the second home it is worth setting up a trust giving him a right to occupy the property, perhaps only at the discretion of the trustees, so that any gain in value during his occupation will qualify for tax relief.

In addition to possible relief from CGT, the owner may be interested in the possibility of saving income tax on any mortgage loan obtained for the purchase of the property. Once again such income tax relief will not normally be available to the owner, or his or her spouse, but if the property is occupied by a dependent relative, rent free, the owner will be able to claim income tax relief on the interest he pays. It may also be possible for mortgage interest to be claimed by another member of the family who wishes to live in the second home. To get such relief the person living in the second home would have to have a share in the ownership, and would himself borrow the money he needed to buy his share. Some form of trust would be necessary, probably a trust for sale, under which the shares owned by each owner would be clearly set out. The person who was to live in the house would then borrow money to pay for his share, and he would be able to claim the relief from income tax on his interest payments. When the property was eventually sold the purchase money would be divided between the owners in the proportions stated in the trust document, and all would benefit from the exemption from CGT.

The other possible method of obtaining some tax relief on the mortgage interest applies only if the property is let to tenants for part of the year. In that case, and provided that the necessary conditions apply to the letting, mortgage interest can be deducted from rent received by the owner thereby saving him tax on the rent. For the mortgage interest to qualify for this tax relief the property must be let on a commercial basis when it is not occupied by the owner and his immediate family. It must be actually let, or available for letting, for at least twenty-six weeks each year.

So that the tenants will not obtain security of tenure (as mentioned in Chapter 11) the best policy is to let the property on short holiday lettings during part of the holiday season, and to let it, or at least advertise it as available for letting, for not more than eight months out of the rest of the year. The owner can then use the property for his own holidays, obtain a high rent during the rest of the holiday season, and if he succeeds in finding a tenant for the rest of the year, obtain some further rent from him. The mortgage interest being paid out of the rent received will reduce the tax payable. Only relief from CGT will be missing.

One other possible problem which the owner of a holiday home may encounter when he lets it is that VAT may have to be charged. Holiday lettings, unlike other lettings of property, are subject to VAT which must be charged by any landlord who is himself registered for VAT. Of course most private owners of holiday homes are not registered for VAT because the income from their lettings is far below the level at which VAT registration becomes necessary. But the problem can arise when the owner is self-employed and himself registered for VAT in connection with his own business. As it is the person owning the business who is registered for VAT, rather than the business itself being registered for VAT, the owner must in that case charge VAT on his holiday lettings also, even though the holiday home has not the slightest connection with the business.

Glossary of legal words and phrases

Beneficial owner: A person entitled to live in, or benefit from, property which is owned under a trust (see Chapter 1).

Beneficiary: Same as beneficial owner.

Chief rent: Similar to ground rent but payable out of freehold rather than leasehold land (see Chapter 2).

Common Law: Ancient law of England, and still the basis of the legal system of England and Wales, as well as most of the States in the U.S.A. and many Commonwealth countries (but not the basis of Scottish law which is a completely different system, based, like that of most European countries, on Roman Law). When William the Conqueror had defeated King Harold he told his new subjects that he would respect their laws. Because there was no formal system of laws operating throughout Saxon England, the Norman Judges, who toured the country hearing cases, compiled a whole system of laws based on the decisions they made. Since then the decisions made by the Courts during the last nine centuries have been the basis of the Common Law.

Covenant: A binding promise or undertaking (see Chapter 3).

Covenantee: The person to whom the promise is made.

Covenantor: The person who made the promise.

Deed: A document transferring legal estates in property or containing covenants (see Chapter 1).

Distraint – (or distress): Collecting overdue rent by taking goods and possessions from the property, usually by sending in the bailiffs.

Easement: A legal right over the land belonging to another person (see Chapter 5).

Feudal system: The system by which land was held by a tenant from his overlord, particularly when he gave military service in return (see Chapter 1).

Ground rent: Rent, usually payable half yearly, attached to long leaseholds (see Chapter 2).

Licence: A right, usually given on a temporary basis, to occupy land, to cross it, to put cables, drains, pipes etc., over or under it, or to carry out some other activity on or over it.

Life tenant (or tenant for life): A person having the right to live in, or receive the rent or other benefit from land which is held under a trust (see Chapter 1).

Matrimonial home: House, flat, or other home belonging to, or rented by, a husband, a wife, or both of them, in which they and the family live.

Mortgagee: The person, company, building society, or other organisation which has loaned money secured by a mortgage.

Nuisance: A legal wrong caused by the occupier or owner of land to his neighbours or the public at large (see Chapter 6).

Owner-occupier: A person who owns a house, flat, or other dwelling, or has the right under a trust to occupy it, who is, or has been in actual occupation. Of particular importance in the case of lettings (see Chapter 11).

Possessory title: Right of ownership gained by long term occupation of property without conflict or opposition (see Chapter 1).

Rack rent: Rent paid under a lease, where the amount paid is the full yearly value of the property (see Chapter 2).

Registration of title: Recording the details of the ownership of a property in HM Land Registry. This registration provides full proof of ownership and replaces the old title deeds.

Remainderman: The person entitled to take over a property when a trust comes to an end.

Statute: Old name for an Act of Parliament. Still used to mean Acts of Parliament, but sometimes meaning other orders made by the Government, or under the authority of Parliament, and having the force of law.

Title: Legal ownership of land as shown by the deeds or in the Land Registry.

Vesting: Transferring the legal ownership to a new owner, or putting it into the name of a new trustee.

Index

Alterations to the home 68–82
Ancient lights 39, 45–46, 49, 55–56
Ancient monuments 78–80
Animals 59
Assignment of a lease 16–17

Bailiff 19–20
Basic amenities, grants for 80–82
Beneficial owner 4, 6
Boundaries 34–41
Building Regulations 68–70, 73–75
Building society 1, 3, 98–99
See also *Mortgage*
Building works 68–82
Burglars 118
Business in the home 126–133

Capital gains tax 135–144
Car parking 71
Caravan 71–72
Change of use 70, 72–73, 126–127
Charge 93–99
Chief rent 18–23
Children, responsibility for 58–59
Common parts of flats 61–62
Compensation for compulsory purchase 84–89
Compulsory purchase 83–89
Conversion of house to flats 72–73, 81, 99
Covenants 26–33, 61, 62–64, 75–77
Creation of rights over property 48–50

Damages 114–115, 123–125
Danger, protection from 121–123
Death of homeowner 11–12
Deed 4–5
Dependent relative 141
Disputes about boundaries 37–38, 40–41
Divorce 11
Drainage 46–47

Easements 42–51
Electricity supply 102
Endowment mortgage 94–95
Enforcement of covenants 31–32, 130–131
Enforcement of rights 50–51
Enfranchisement of a lease 23–25, 64
Entail 8
Extension of lease 25
Extensions 68–82

Fences 34–41
Feudal system 1–4, 10, 11–12, 14
Flats 43, 60–67, 72–73
Flying freehold 62–63
Freehold 14, 23–25, 28–31, 62–64
Fumes 53–55

Garden 138–140
Gas supply 102
General rates 99–102, 133
Grants 80–82
Green belt 92
Ground rent 16–22
Guests 58–59, 119, 121–123

Hedges 34–41
Highways 56–57, 72, 89–90
Historic buildings 78–80
Holiday home 107–109, 142–144
Husband and wife 9–11, 140–141

Improvement grants 80–82
Improvement works 68–82
Insulation grants 82
Insurance 102–104, 123
Intruder 113–118, 122–123

Joint owners 6, 9–11

Land Charges Registry 10
Land Registry 5, 6, 10, 35
Lease, covenants in 27–28
Leasehold 15–17, 23–25, 62–64
Letting 105–111
Licensing laws 132
Life tenant 7–9, 141
Light 39, 45–46, 49, 55–56
Listed buildings 78–80
Lodgers 73, 111–112
London Building Acts 68–70, 73–75

MIRAS 98
Management of blocks of flats 64–67
Marriage breakdown 11
Matrimonial proceedings 11
Mortgages 93–99
Multiple occupation 73, 81

Negligence 123–125
Noise 53–55
Non-payment of mortgage 98–99
Nuisance 52–59, 60–61, 124–125

Occupiers liability 121–125
Oil tank 71
Owner-occupier letting home 105–111
Ownership 1–13

Part of home let 110–111
Party walls 36–37
Pets 59
Planning applications by others 77–78

Planning blight 89
Planning permission 68–73
Planning restrictions 39, 126–128
Pollution control 91–92
Porch 71
Positive covenants 28–33, 37
Possessory title 12–13, 34–35, 38
Probate 12
Public inquiry 85

Rate rebate 100
Rateable value 99–100
Rates 99–102
Registration of land 5, 6, 10, 35
Remainderman 8, 9
Rent 16–22
Rentcharge 18–23
Repairs 37–38, 44–45
Restrictive covenants 28–33, 39, 75–77, 128–131
Retirement home 109–110
Rights attaching to property 42–51
Rights of light 39, 45–46, 49, 55–56
Rights of support 47
Rights of way 43–45, 48–51, 120
Roads 56–57, 72, 89–90

Safety 121–125
Second home 107–109, 142–144
Secret trust 7
Service charges 61–62, 66
Sewers 47
Shared driveway 44–45, 48
Slum clearance 83–84
Smells 53–55
Smoke 53–55, 91–92
Spouses 9–11, 140–141
Squatters rights 12–13
Sublease 16–17, 20–22
Support 47

T marks 36

Tax relief for business 133
Tax reliefs for homeowners 95–98, 135–144
Telephone 102
Tenancy of home, granting 105–111
Tenant for life 7–9, 141
Trees 55–58, 92
Trespass 113–118, 122–123
Trusts 3–10

Use, change of 70, 72–73, 126–127

Valuation appeal 100–101
Vibrations 53–55
Visitors 58–59, 119, 121–123

Walls 34–41
Water 46–47
Water rates 101–102, 133
Wife 9–11, 140–141
Will 12
Working at home 126–133
Workmen, responsibility for 58–59